Missing Persons

What Happens When Someone Disappears?

By Amanda Vink

Portions of this book originally appeared in
Missing Persons by Gail B. Stewart.

LUCENT
P R E S S

Published in 2018 by
Lucent Press, an Imprint of Greenhaven Publishing, LLC
353 3rd Avenue
Suite 255
New York, NY 10010

Designer: Deanna Paternostro
Editor: Jennifer Lombardo

Cataloging-in-Publication Data

Names: Vink, Amanda.
Title: Missing persons: what happens when someone disappears? / Amanda Vink
Description: New York : Lucent Press, 2018. | Series: Crime scene investigations | Includes index.
Identifiers: ISBN 9781534562752 (pbk.) | ISBN 9781534561786 (library bound) | ISBN 9781534561779
(ebook)
Subjects: LCSH: Missing persons–Juvenile literature. | Disappeared persons–Juvenile literature. |
Missing children–Juvenile literature.
Classification: LCC HV6762.A3 V56 2018 | DDC 362.8–dc23

Printed in the United States of America

CPSIA compliance information: Batch #CW18KL: For further information contact Greenhaven Publishing LLC, New York, New York at 1-844-317-7404.

Please visit our website, www.greenhavenpublishing.com. For a free color catalog of all our
high-quality books, call toll free 1-844-317-7404 or fax 1-844-317-7405.

Contents

Foreword

For decades, popular television programs and movies have depicted the life and work of police officers, detectives, and crime scene investigators. Many of these shows and films portray forensic scientists as the brains responsible for cracking cases and bringing criminals to justice. Undoubtedly, these crime scene analysts are an important part in the process of crime solving. With modern technology and advances in forensic analysis, these highly trained experts are a crucial component of law enforcement systems all across the world.

Police officers and detectives are also integral members of the law enforcement team. They are the ones who respond to 911 calls about crime, collect physical evidence, and use their high level of training to identify suspects and culprits. They work right alongside forensic investigators to figure out the mysteries behind why a crime is committed, and the entire team cooperates to gather enough evidence to convict someone in a court of law.

Ever since the first laws were recorded, crime scene investigation has been handled in roughly the same way. An authority is informed that a crime has been committed; someone looks around the crime scene and interviews potential witnesses; suspects are identified based on evidence and testimony; and, finally, someone is formally accused of committing a crime. This basic plan is generally effective, and criminals are often caught and brought to justice. Throughout history, however, certain limitations have sometimes prevented authorities from finding out who was responsible for a crime.

There are many reasons why a crime goes unsolved: Maybe a dead body was found too late, evidence was tampered with, or witnesses lied. Sometimes, even the greatest technology of the age is simply not good enough to process and analyze the evidence at a crime scene. In the United States during the 20th century, for example, the person responsible for the infamous Zodiac killings was never found, despite the earnest efforts of hundreds of policemen, detectives, and forensic analysts.

In modern times, science and technology are integral to the investigative process. From DNA analysis to high-definition surveillance video, it has become much more difficult to commit a crime and get away with it. Using advanced computers and immense databases, microscopic skin cells from a crime scene can be collected and then analyzed by a forensic scientist, leading detectives to the home of the culprit of a crime. Dozens of people work behind the scenes of criminal investigations to figure out the unique and complex elements of a crime. Although this process is still time-consuming and complicated, technology is constantly improving and adapting to the needs of police forces worldwide.

This series is designed to help young readers understand the systems in place to allow forensic professionals to do their jobs. Covering a wide range of topics, from the assassination of President John F. Kennedy to 21st-century cybercriminals, these titles describe in detail the ways in which technology and criminal investigations have evolved over more than 50 years. They cite eyewitnesses and experts in order to give a detailed and nuanced picture of the difficult task of rooting out criminals. Although television shows and movies add drama to the crime scene investigation process, these real-life stories have enough drama on their own. This series sticks to the facts surrounding some of the highest-profile criminal cases of the modern era and the people who work to solve them and other crimes every day.

Introduction

Danger

Statistics of missing persons are hard to pin down. Some experts say a child goes missing every 40 seconds; others are more skeptical and argue the problem is not as large as the studies claim it to be. Although statistics are important and can reveal a lot about this issue, there are a few things of which an informed individual should be aware. Most information collected in studies of missing persons involves the number of reports. For example, if one child is reported missing five times in a year, each individual time is counted. On the other hand, there are many instances when someone goes missing and it is not reported to the police. The numbers used in this book are based upon the most reliable data, which inarguably shows that the number of reports of missing persons is very large. On average, there are roughly 90,000 people missing at any given time in the United States.

However, it is important to note that violent crime in the United States has been decreasing despite the perception that society is becoming more violent and crime-ridden. According to FBI statistics, the violent crime rate per 100,000 residents fell 50 percent between 1993 and 2015.

However, people do go missing, and missing persons can be in danger. Whether a person goes missing from an accident or a violent crime, it is crucial that an investigation begins right away. Advances in procedures and forensic science have given the police more information to find the missing. A timely and thorough investigation gives the best chance for the missing to come home to safety.

Going Missing

Some people go missing by accident and are generally found a short time later; for example, little children and people with Alzheimer's disease may wander away from home and become confused about how to get back. Dangerous

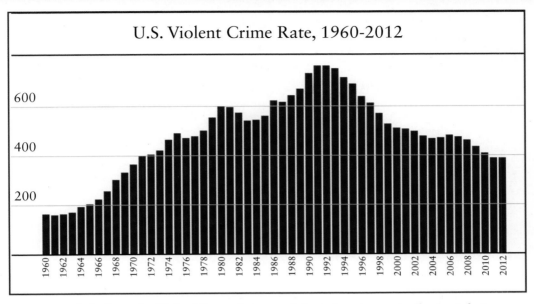

U.S. Violent Crime Rate, 1960-2012

Many people believe the United States is more violent than it was in the past, but the violent crime rate has actually been decreasing, as this information from The Atlantic *shows. This graph charts the number of violent crimes per 100,000 residents.*

environmental disasters such as earthquakes or tsunamis can scatter residents, and often rescue teams work day and night to find the missing among the rubble that remains.

Others go missing on purpose—runaways who do not feel safe or welcome in their homes or teens who are angry and rebel at the rules their parents or guardians set down. In some cases, they, too, come back within a day or two. However, a spontaneous breaking of the rules can lead to danger, and what begins as a voluntary getaway sometimes becomes life threatening. In one such case, a teen named Monique agreed, against her mother's wishes, to

go to a party with her older boyfriend, Shawn. She expected to return later that night, but when Shawn and his friends started drinking, they sexually assaulted Monique. She was held in the apartment against her will for two days.

The most dangerous missing persons cases are the kidnappings, or abductions, in which a person is taken forcefully. Many times the victim is sexually assaulted or murdered. Police know that too many times in such cases, what starts as a rescue mission becomes one of recovering a victim's body. Many such bodies have been recovered—experts estimate that the unidentified remains of as many as

40,000 men, women, and children lie in morgues or have been buried or cremated to make room for more. Roughly 4,400 unidentified human bodies are brought in every year.

Investigators do their best to locate all missing persons. The sheer volume of missing persons cases is daunting, however—so much so that the National Missing and Unidentified Persons System, or NamUs, called the number of missing "our country's silent mass disaster."[1] However, with a variety of scientific instruments and strategies to help them, law enforcement, forensic workers, search and rescue teams, and sometimes even volunteers dedicate themselves to finding the missing.

Chapter One

Gone

There is a common misconception that one full day needs to pass before a missing person report can be filed. In fact, according to adjunct professor of criminal justice and former NYPD sergeant Joseph L. Giacalone, "The ... biggest problem is that family members wait too long to report a missing persons case. You lose valuable time during those 24 hours."[2]

Police often get their first notification of a missing person through a 911 call. Cathe Carbone, an emergency dispatcher who handles 911 calls for Ramsey County, Minnesota, said missing persons calls come in on a regular basis. "We're the first ones a family talks to, and most of the time—especially when it's a missing child—the caller is understandably frightened and panicked. You can hear it in their voice. They're almost incoherent—just holding on by a thread," she said. "So we need to get the mother or father or whoever is calling to calm down enough so that we can get

the important information."[3]

"I always start out by telling them that help is on the way," Carbone continued. She has learned that it is helpful for the caller to know that they are not alone. "And it also helps to give them something to focus on other than their fear—especially if the missing person is a young child. I ask them questions about the child—what he or she was wearing last, whether it's possible that the child could be in the neighborhood with a friend."[4]

Staying positive is an important part of Carbone's job. The parent needs to hear that the child will be found soon. "It really does make a difference to proceed that way," she said:

Most missing children are found very quickly, so parents need to hear that. I have them give me the name of their dog or cat that the child might recognize right away. I say, "You know, when the officers

An important part of a 911 dispatcher's job is keeping callers calm.

find your little girl, they don't want to scare her—it helps if they can say, 'Hey, aren't you the one with a dog named Sparky?' or something like that." Kids often get frightened when strangers—even police officers—approach them, so hearing their pet's name makes them less scared. And talking about a good outcome helps the parents, too.[5]

First Response

While the dispatcher is talking with the caller, a number of other things are happening. Chris Stark of the Saint Paul, Minnesota, Police Department's Missing Persons Unit described a typical call:

Let's say a six-year-old is missing. While the dispatcher is talking to that caller, she's also sending a marked squad to the home. In addition, she's calling the Missing Persons Unit. She tells me, "I've got a missing six-year-old, mother's on the line. I'll patch you through." So as the squad's en route, I'm talking to the mother, and I have some questions I ask her right away.[6]

One of the missing persons detective's first jobs is to ensure that the child is entered into the FBI's National Crime Information Center's (NCIC) computerized database. The NCIC database was started on January 27, 1967, with 356,784 records. By the end of 2015, it contained 12 million active records. It is available to every law enforcement office in the United States. "Most likely, the child has simply wandered off in the neighborhood," said Stark, "and when that child is found, the information is deleted. But it's good to have it entered immediately, in case it ends up turning into something far more serious, such as an abduction."[7]

Stark said his job, once the dispatcher has patched him through to the person reporting the missing child, is to ask very specific questions:

I get the basics—the age, weight, race, description of what the child is wearing and if he or she has any scars or any missing teeth. If I'm talking to the dad, I ask about the mother and if there's a chance the child could be with her, or if there is conflict in the home. Are there custody issues? That can happen sometimes, where the noncustodial parent grabs the child. And I ask if there was anybody outside who saw anything—if any other kids saw him or her leave.[8]

Gathering Information

Once he gets the information entered into the NCIC database, Stark goes to the home. Patrol officers will have arrived by that time, and they ask questions, too. "You know, someone might say, 'Isn't that a lot of the same questions being asked?' I'd agree," he said. "And that's by design [on purpose]."[9]

Stark said that if foul play is involved—if a parent is responsible for the disappearance of the child—the accounts that parent gives will likely have discrepancies, or slight differences. "It's not as easy as you might think to lie—you have to keep so many details straight so you don't contradict yourself later on," he said. "And if a parent says one thing to me, and something different later on, that could be important."[10]

Investigators are aware that the questions they need to ask can make parents feel defensive. Police know the importance of never sounding as if they are suggesting that the disappearance is the parents' fault. "There are families who have a different style of parenting," Stark said. "They may be comfortable with letting very young children head down to the park on their own, for instance. So when I ask, 'When is the last time you checked on your child?' they might get defensive. So looking as though I'm passing judgment on them as parents won't do any good."[11]

Assuming investigators have not heard or sensed anything that indicates that the child has been abducted or harmed, they proceed with their standard search protocol. "When you're talking about a young child, a preschooler, it's important to find that child quickly, because they're extremely vulnerable," Stark said. "So we look at the most likely places they'd be—which starts with the home itself. And that can make people very nervous."[12]

In some neighborhoods, many parents are also hesitant to allow police to come inside their home to search. "I say, 'Look, I'm not here to judge you. Right now I don't care if you are making [drugs] in the basement, or if you've got a money printing operation going on in the bedroom,'" Stark said. "I tell them I'm not here about anything like that—I just say that I'm here to find their child."[13]

By the Numbers

88,040

active entries in the NCIC Database as of December 31, 2016

Saint Paul patrol officer Brady Harrison knows from experience the importance of having first responders search the home, even when parents insist that they have already searched it. In one instance, he was called to a house on the east side of the city, where a woman had tearfully reported her three-year-old boy missing.

"I got there, and she said she'd been looking for him for the past 20 minutes," Harrison recalled. "He was in his crib taking a nap, and when she checked on him she discovered he wasn't there. The doors were all unlocked, she checked the house, the yard, and even the neighbors, but there wasn't any sign of him. Anyway, she was hysterical, thinking the worst had happened."[14]

Harrison explained that he asked the mother a number of routine questions:

I wanted to know if she'd checked the basement really thoroughly— looked in the dryer, under piles of clothes, that kind of thing. I asked if he ever walked over to the neighbor kids' houses, and she said, yes, he'd done that a few times. So we went out and talked to the neighbors again. I sent them to check their houses carefully—everybody seemed to have unlocked doors, so maybe the little kid just let himself in, and nobody noticed.[15]

While the neighbors agreed to search their houses, Harrison told the mother that the two of them would search her house again, top to bottom.

When we got to the little boy's room, I noticed that his crib had one of those valances—the material that hangs down so it kind of blinds the space underneath. Anyway, I got down and looked under the crib, and there he was—sound asleep. Like being in a little tent, I guess. Anyway, the mother just started sobbing, she was so relieved. It just shows how important it is to check the home first.[16]

Using Grid Searches

In cases where investigators have searched the house and yard without success, they organize what is called a grid search. They take a neighborhood map and divide it into smaller segments. Then, each patrol car (as many as the missing persons investigator thinks are needed for the area) makes methodical passes through each segment.

"Basically, the squad car is going north, then south, then north, then south—through that whole segment," Stark

To perform a grid search, investigators take a map of the neighborhood and divide it into small segments that are methodically searched.

explained. "Then the officers get to the end of the area, and then they go east, then west, then east, then west. They're going very slowly—through alleys as well as on the streets, looking in backyards where a child might be. If they see an open garage door or something like that, cops don't need a warrant, they stop and take a look."[17]

Stark explained that even in the roughest, most crime-ridden neighborhoods, people are very cooperative when it comes to a missing child. "When a child goes missing, almost everyone is on the same page. Everybody's got kids, and this can happen in any family. Everybody is willing to help. And that's why most of the time, these children are found very quickly."[18]

Urgent Matters

Unfortunately, some cases do not end happily—and these cases highlight the sense of urgency police have in finding a missing child. One example occurred in Mamakating, New York, in February 2009. The parents of three-year-old Cassandra Weronick called police at 7:00 a.m. Cassandra was missing, and the front door was open. The toddler had wandered out of the house before, but her parents had been able to find her very quickly. This time they could find no sign of her. Their sense of urgency was even

greater because the temperature was in the single digits, and Cassandra had been wearing only a T-shirt and a diaper.

Very soon after taking the information about the missing child, police received another call. A woman on her way to work had seen what she thought was a doll on the side of the road, about half a mile from the Weronicks' home. She stopped to look more closely and realized it was the lifeless body of a little girl. The body was identified as Cassandra's. She had died of exposure to the bitter cold. "There's not too much you can say about it other than it's a sad, sad event,"[19] said former state police captain Wayne Olson.

Missing by Accident

As frightening and potentially tragic as a missing child case can be, children are not the only ones who disappear. Abductions and runaways aside, many adults go missing every day, and they are sometimes in grave danger, too. One example is the case of 19-year-old Brandon Swanson, who vanished in rural southwest Minnesota in May 2008.

Brandon was driving home from a party at about midnight after celebrating the end of his freshman year of college. However, he took a wrong turn on a country road and ended up in a

"Brandon's Law"

For Annette and Brian Swanson, one of the most frustrating aspects of their son's disappearance was the slow response by the police. When Annette Swanson called the police department in Lynd, Minnesota, at 6:30 a.m. after she and her husband had been searching all night, the police told her it was not uncommon for a 19-year-old to go missing once in a while. One officer told her that as an adult, Brandon had a right to go missing.

That angered the Swansons because the circumstances of Brandon's disappearance were troubling. They lobbied for a law that would expand Minnesota's missing children's law to include adults who are missing and could be in danger. Named "Brandon's Law," it was passed on May 7, 2009, and it requires Minnesota police to take a report immediately, no matter what the missing person's age, and conduct a preliminary investigation to see if the person is in danger.

ditch. Using his cell phone, he called his parents, telling them exactly where he was and that he needed a ride. Annette and Brian Swanson quickly set out to pick up their son.

When they got to the place where Brandon said he was, his parents could find no trace of him or his car. However, they continued to speak to him by cell phone, so they were not terribly concerned. "We were saying, 'We're flashing our lights!'"[20] his mother recalled. Over the phone they could hear Brandon doing the same, clicking his own lights off and on. Brandon asked, "Don't you see me?"[21]

At one point, he became frustrated and impatient with his parents. He finally said he was just going to walk back to his friend's house. As he walked, he continued to talk to his father on the cell, telling him where he was. However, after a 46-minute conversation, during which his parents were still unable to find any sign of him, the cell phone suddenly went dead. Did something happen to Swanson to make him break the connection so abruptly? That question could not be answered. Though his parents continued throughout the night to look for their son, they had no success.

Modern Technology

A whole range of tools can be used to search for a person missing in physically challenging terrain, such as farm country or wilderness areas. Some of these tools involve cutting-edge

In order to receive service, a cell phone connects to a cell tower similar to this one. Investigators can use data from multiple cell towers to determine a person's location.

technology, while others are methods that have been used for centuries. It was modern technology that helped law enforcement find Brandon's car.

Though Brandon had told his parents he was close to the town of Lynd, Minnesota, where he had been partying with friends, the Swansons and police had found no sign of his car. Perhaps, investigators thought, he had taken a wrong turn and was not in Lynd at all. To check his location at the time he made the calls to his parents, police contacted his cell phone company. Each time a person makes a cell phone call, the location of the phone is automatically noted.

In this case, the cell phone company's records showed that the calls to his parents that night had originated more than 25 miles (40.2 km) northwest of Lynd, in Porter, Minnesota. That is where they found the car—off an access road to a farmer's field near Porter. Although Brandon was not in the car, it provided police with a starting place to begin their search.

Using Science

Once searchers have a last known position (LKP), other high-tech tools help them track the person. According to Minnesota-based search and rescue expert Ken Anderson, an investigation such as the Swanson search relies on multiple methods. He uses a lot of portable communications equipment, along with hand-held devices with programs that can display weather maps, black-and-white satellite photos of an area, and the geological layout of an area. He said, "Those maps are really helpful, especially in a rural search area. You want to know where the creeks and rivers are, the ditches, any area that might be especially dangerous to someone walking at night. You can check what the weather conditions were on the night he went missing, and the possible dangers of hypothermia, for example."[22]

Anderson said what his group does is hard to define. "What we do isn't one specific science," he explained, "but it's a very artful way of using sciences. You need to understand a bunch of disciplines—meteorology, geography, geology—when you're doing a search like this."[23]

Once Brandon's car was located, Anderson and others used mathematical calculations to determine how far he might have walked in the time he was walking and talking to his father. "We had no idea what direction he was going," Anderson said, "so we ended up with a large area—a ring of about 122 square miles."[24]

Next Steps

Police were disappointed to find no visible clues in or near the car that

Training Dogs to Search

Dogs trained for search and rescue (SAR) alert their handlers to the scent of skin cells—the thousands of them that the body sheds constantly. However, when a person dies, those cells are no longer being shed, and the smell of decomposition overpowers anything else. When searchers believe they are no longer looking for a living person, they use cadaver dogs, trained to alert their handlers to the scent of human decay.

"They won't be interested in the smell of a dead rabbit or a rotten fish on the riverbank," said Sarah Ryan, a Colorado handler.

> *When we train them, we train them very specifically. That means just human smell. Even minute [tiny] amounts from skeletal remains that we can't smell, they can. I've seen lots of dogs that can even smell a dead body underwater—they ride in a boat and alert [the handler] by barking when they get close. You've got to see it to believe it.*[1]

Many cadaver dogs are trained at a facility in North Carolina. Western Carolina University's Forensic Osteology Research Station (FOReSt)—which is sometimes also called a "body farm" because it is where researchers study the decomposition of bodies—exposes dogs to bodies in different states of decomposition to help improve their ability to find human remains.

1. Sarah Ryan, telephone interview by Gail B. Stewart, June 15, 2010.

Cadaver dogs can smell a body submerged in water or buried under several feet of dirt.

indicated which direction Brandon went from there. "There's grass in the ditch and gravel on the road," recalled retired Lincoln County sheriff Jack Vizecky, "so it's possible to leave that vehicle and not leave any tracks."[25]

Because of the sheer size of the area, law enforcement brought in a search and rescue (SAR) group, which included experienced tracking dog handlers. SAR dogs are different from police K-9 teams because they are trained to follow the scent of a particular individual. "Our handlers get an article of clothing or something else that would have the person's scent on it—it could be a sock, a T-shirt, a pillowcase,"[26] Anderson explained.

A human sheds thousands of dead skin cells every day, and though humans cannot smell them, tracking dogs can. In this case, all the dogs were given small items belonging to Brandon to smell, and with their handlers, they began tracking the young man's path. The dogs followed his scent to a wooded area near the banks of the Yellow Medicine River. Some investigators thought Brandon could have fallen into the river, the depth of which ranges from 18 inches (45 cm) in some areas to over 15 feet (4.5 m).

However, other investigators are convinced that if that had occurred, his body would have been carried downstream. Vizecky said that thorough searches along more than 2 miles (3.2 km) of riverbank found no trace of him.

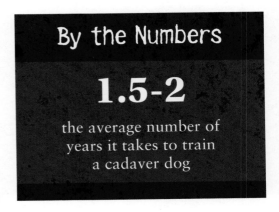

By the Numbers

1.5-2

the average number of years it takes to train a cadaver dog

A Recovery Case

After a while, little possibility remained of finding Brandon alive. Police called off their investigation, and the case's status turned to recovery. As of January 2017, volunteer rescue and recovery crews are still looking for him.

"The idea, once it gets to that point, is that you want to find the body, so you can provide a true answer," said Sarah Ryan, a Colorado woman who does SAR work with her dog Gus. "Even if it is not the answer we want—if the person missing is no longer alive, it's still an answer. And all the people who loved that person have that much, at least, so they're not in limbo, thinking about it all the time."[27]

In the case of Brandon Swanson, crews keep searching, using cadaver dogs that are trained to be alert to the scent of human remains—even small bits of remains, such as bones or teeth. As of January 2017, the crews have operated 1,900 K-9 missions with 45 trained dogs with the purpose of finding Brandon. Crews continue to search the creeks and the Yellow Medicine River, hoping to provide an answer to a family that has waited so long.

Chapter Two
Deliberately Missing

Many people who vanish disappear on purpose. These people, most of whom are children and young adults, either leave voluntarily or are thrown out of their homes. Experts estimate that between 1.6 million and 2.8 million young people run away each year. Some of these individuals have a plan and maybe an alternative place to stay, but many more do not. In some of these cases, a runaway may come home after a few days. Others may come back after a few months. Other times, a runaway may never return.

Why Children and Young Adults Leave

Kids and teens run away for a variety of reasons. Sometimes they run away from problems faced at home or at school. Some leave because they are angry at parental restrictions they feel are unfair. Maya, a Wisconsin teen, ran away in 2007 when she was 15. "Looking back, I was a pretty angry kid," she said.

I was mad at my parents because they tried to restrict my dating. I was going out with a boy they didn't like because he was four years older than me. My mom and stepfather told me he was off limits. I ended up staying with the friend of a friend from work for almost a month before I decided to go back. We did family counseling, and it helped us get along better— listen to each other better, I guess you'd say.[28]

The National Runaway Safeline (NRS), formerly known as the National Runaway Switchboard, is the federally designated national telephone line dedicated to helping youth who are homeless or considering running away. Findings from the organization's 2010 report revealed that 29 percent of children and young adults leave home because of family problems, including divorce, remarriage, and problems with siblings. This was the largest reason given by callers.

Ann Rivera, a family counselor, said an increasing number of minors leave because their home lives are toxic—generally through no fault of their own:

> Some are escaping violence in the home, or parents who do not understand them. We see lots of families where there is a lot of drug and alcohol abuse. So many parents are angry, and though the children are not to blame, they're often the ones that the parents target with that anger. And one day, the child maybe thinks, "I've had

> enough," and the next day after school or whatever, he or she just doesn't come home.[29]

Many children and young adults are cast out by their parents or caregivers. Forty-eight percent of the kids who were interviewed by the NRS in Los Angeles, California, and Chicago, Illinois, said they were thrown out of their homes. Inspector Mike Sullivan of the Minneapolis Police Department's Juvenile Unit said he and his officers see the same thing, day after day:

> So many families are in shambles— that's the best way I can think of to say it. They're just broken. No one is looking out for the kids. And sometimes we see kids that don't

LGBT+ Youth Homelessness by the Numbers

youth population

5-10% LGBT+

homeless youth population

20-40% LGBT+

Although only 5 percent to 10 percent of young adults are LGBT+, they experience homelessness at much higher rates than other young adults, as this information from the Center for American Progress shows.

just run once—we've had kids as young as 11 or 12 that take off 10, 15 times in a 6-month period. Once, you think, well, it's a one-time thing, and they'll work it out. Ten or 15 times—you know something really serious is going on there.[30]

Children and teens may also leave because they do not feel accepted by their communities for various reasons. Many young adults suffer from bullying at school. The LGBT+ community is especially affected: Of youths who have run away or been thrown out, 20 to 40 percent identify as part of the LGBT+ community.

A Great Danger

Police admit that in the past, many departments did not take runaways very seriously. "There really wasn't much of a sense of urgency about it," said Sullivan. "The way cops used to handle it was, 'Hey, we'll see if the juvenile shows up in a couple of days.' That's probably because a lot of time, that's all it took, and a runaway would come home on his or her own."[31]

However, that thinking has changed. Many runaways end up homeless, and police know it is not uncommon for them to turn to illegal activities such as drug dealing and prostitution as a way to support themselves on the street. Homeless youth have a higher risk factor for diseases such as HIV and AIDS. Being homeless also makes it more difficult for them to receive adequate health care. Police know runaways are in far greater danger of being injured or killed in an accident, sexually assaulted, or murdered than other young people. For these reasons and others, taking a "wait and see" attitude about runaways is frequently risky.

Missing persons officers Stark and Benny Williams had a 2009 case in which two young teenage girls ran away. "They had come up here [to Minnesota] with their foster mother—didn't really know anybody," Williams said. "They were from North Carolina someplace and were just hoping to have some excitement up here in the city. But the girls ran off from the foster mother, who called us to report them missing. What happened was, they got picked up by two older guys and taken across the river to Minneapolis."[32]

"We tracked them down," Stark added, "but not before one of the girls had been raped nine times. Running can be really risky business—a lot of these kids just don't get that. The streets can be a dangerous place. That's why it's important for us to get a jump on these cases, and find these kids before they get into more trouble than they can handle."[33]

Many runaways turn to illegal activities such as prostitution as a way to support themselves on the street.

Legal Consequences

In nine states, running away under the age of majority is illegal, and police can force a minor to return home. The age of majority is 18 except in Alabama, Nebraska, and Mississippi; in Alabama and Nebraska it is 19, and in Mississippi it is 21. In some states where running away is not illegal, a minor who is found by police may still be required to speak to a judge about their reasons for leaving home. Even in these states, a minor who is found by police may be forced to return home if the parents want them to and if the police believe the person does not have a good reason—or, in legal terms, "just cause"—for running away.

Some states protect a runaway's legal rights. In Maine, for instance, police who find a runaway may take them into what is known as interim care. This is a safe place for the person to stay for up to six hours while police learn the circumstances of the situation. They will call the runaway's parents and see if both the parents and the runaway are willing to have the runaway return home. If one of them does not want this to happen, the Department of Health and Human Services (DHHS) will be called to decide where to place the runaway. A minor cannot live on their own because in many cases, laws prevent them from getting a job, an apartment, and other important resources. However, a DHHS worker can help the runaway find a safe place to stay where they will be taken care of, such as a shelter. If the DHHS worker believes the young adult will be unsafe at home, they will most likely not force the person to return.

If the person is already in a safe place, such as a friend or relative's house, the police may not do anything further. However, sometimes the police try to force a runaway to return home even if they do not want to go back. If this happens, there are legal resources a young adult can turn to for help.

Not all states protect runaways the way Maine does. In some places, a runaway can be forced to return home even if the situation there is dangerous for them. Additionally, in some states, anyone who lets a runaway stay in their house without the permission of the runaway's parents can be arrested as well. This is known as harboring a runaway.

Getting Photographs

One of the first steps in a runaway investigation is to obtain a recent photograph of the runaway. While that sounds like an easy task, police say it frequently is very difficult. Parents of runaways may not have or may not be able to locate a recent photo.

Sullivan said his department gets a great deal of help from the School Resource Officers (SROs). These are Minneapolis police officers who are assigned to the junior highs and high schools throughout the city. "Those photos are critical," he said, "and that's where the SROs come in handy. They can immediately get the administration to give them a school photo. The cops then can get it duplicated and handed out to all officers throughout the metro area. And if the runaway is an at-risk kid, that photo will go out on television, too."[34]

Looking at Cell Phone Records

Another technology that can help police track down runaways more quickly is a cell phone. "If the child or teen has a cell phone, chances are they're in touch with friends," said Mark, who asked that his last name not be used. His 16-year-old daughter ran away several years ago. "We found her by calling our cell phone provider, and they got numbers she had called," he said. "We were lucky that the numbers we called were answered by her friends who were willing to help us."[35]

Mark said that by talking to more than 12 people, they were able to find out she had run to Chicago, nearly 600 miles (965 km) away. "We learned bits and pieces, and contacted the police, who were able to find her," he said. "She was gone more than

Runaway Adults

While the majority of runaways reported each year are minors (under the age of 18), police say adults go missing on purpose, too. Stark recalled being contacted by an older woman who reported her husband missing. She was worried that he might have fallen on the ice and bumped his head and ended up in a hospital somewhere.

"I took her information," Stark said, "got his social security number, his photo, checked around where he had worked. Well, I found out he'd applied for a job in Phoenix. It turned out he was an abused husband—his wife beat him up." When Stark got in touch with the man and asked if he had been abused by his wife, the man verified that he had. "I told him I understood, and I hoped his life worked out well. I called the wife back, told her he was alive, and that I'd learned there was more to the story than she'd told me."[1]

1. Chris Stark, interview by Gail B. Stewart, May 27, 2010.

six weeks but ended up okay. Without those [cell phone] records, we'd never have known who to talk to."[36]

Bank Cards and Video Footage

Bank records, too, can be of great help to investigators. Sullivan explained,

If the runaway has a bank card—and a lot of kids do—bank records can trace any activity on the card. If they're making withdrawals or using it, we'll know by the locations [where] they're using it whether they're still in town. And if they're not, we'll know that, too. To make sure the card is being used by the runaway and not by someone else, we'll call the bank and ask them to send us video of the time and location the card was used. Our officers are really good at that—they go through the video frame by frame, making sure it's the kid we're looking for.[37]

Film or video is helpful in other ways, too. Sullivan recalled a case of an 11-year-old runaway. "He was young, so definitely an at-risk runaway," he said. "But in terms of just savvy and intelligence, he was really good at being on his own. He knew every street, every bus, how to get everywhere on light rail … It seemed like we were never there at the right time to catch up to him."[38]

Police officers had talked to some people who knew the boy and learned that he was spending at least part of the

*Missing persons investigators can use video
surveillance film to help track down the missing.*

day at the Mall of America. They contacted the transit company and asked for video surveillance tapes from several of the bus lines. "And there he was," Sullivan said. "We got an idea of when he was using those buses, and that's how we caught up with him. Just another young kid whose parents aren't paying any attention to him."[39]

Doing the Legwork

While technological tools can be of great help in finding runaways, investigators say it is simply determination that solves most cases. According to Stark, "Most of our cases get solved by going out and looking, talking to people, looking in spots we know that kid usually hangs out."[40]

One of the first places a police officer will check is the runaway's school. "I guess it sounds surprising," Sullivan said, "but a lot of kids who run actually show up in class. A lot of it is probably because their friends are there. But school provides some structure to their day—and a hot meal, too. They may not make it every day, but more often than you might think."[41]

Another important step is talking with friends of the person who has run away. Police know that young people with problems are almost always more likely to confide in their friends than family members or other adults. However, getting a friend to talk is not

Missing persons investigators can use a person's cell phone to gain valuable information and leads from friends.

at all like interrogating a suspect in a crime, Stark said:

If you approach it that way, you'll walk out with nothing. I think it helps if you generally care about whomever it is that's missing. I'll go up to his school, ask around— let's say it's a 16-year-old boy. I talk to a teacher or counselor and ask who the kid's closest friends are, and I'll talk to them. But it's just talk—I'm not asking a bunch of questions and demanding that they answer them.[42]

Stark said he begins by asking questions that may reveal a motive for running away. "I ask if he [was] worried about anything in particular, or if he was in love with someone. Any of these things could have something to do with why the kid ran away."[43]

By the Numbers

15-17

average age of a runaway
in the United States

Because police know young people often confide in friends, they do extensive legwork trying to contact and talk to all friends of the missing.

Winning Confidences

Stark knows that generally friends want to be helpful, but they are very reluctant to give away secrets—either their friend's or their own. "I mean, you've got kids who've been smoking a little pot, or drinking illegally with the runaway. I tell them, 'Look, this isn't about you. I'm not interested in arresting you for anything,'"[44] he said.

Stark has become good at reading body language—an important part of any police interview. "I can tell when they're stalling," he said. "I watch how they avoid looking me in the eye. I watch the way they move in the chair, and how when you ask something sensitive they kind of close down, you know? I say, 'Did you guys smoke some pot together?' And they say, 'Um, no, not really.' [It's] not too hard to tell they're nervous."[45]

Police understand the reluctance a teen might feel about talking about his or her missing friend, but knowing about the teen's motives can give the police a place to start looking. This is important because the sooner the runaway is found, the less chance they have to get into a dangerous situation. Stark said he understands how the runaway's friends feel:

I was a kid once, too. Cops are the same way—we don't want to squeal on each other. There's a code. But by closing ranks, by being silent and trying to protect your friend, you're not hurting the police, you're ultimately hurting your friend. I tell [the runaway's] friends—"Call me on the phone, don't even give your name, I don't care. I just want to get him home safe."[46]

A polygraph machine similar to this one may be used by investigators to determine whether someone is lying.

By the Numbers

33,388

number of missing persons under 18 as of 2014

Using an Anonymous Tip

Some runaway cases have been solved by an anonymous tip. One was the highly publicized disappearance of 17-year-old Abbi Obermiller of North Fairfield, Ohio. When she ran away on June 7, 2010, her parents were certain she had gone to be with her boyfriend, a 20-year-old named Bobby Young. They had disapproved of Abbi seeing him because they believed he was possessive and controlling. "He didn't even want her near her friends during the prom," her mother, Rose, recalled. "She had this

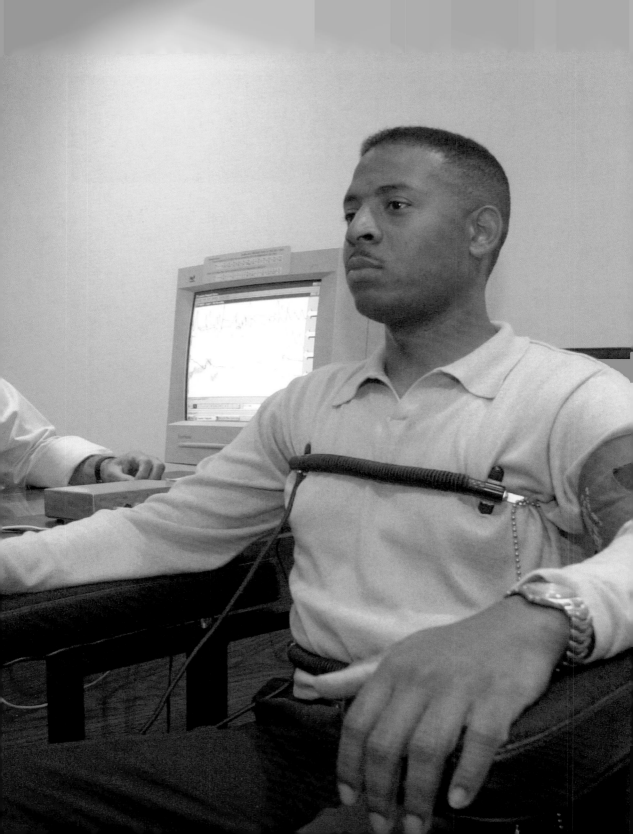

Occupation: Missing Persons Investigator

Job Description:
Missing persons investigators look for clues and evidence to locate people who have gone missing. Sometimes this means working long hours, especially in a time-sensitive case where the missing person may be in danger. They may be required to interrogate suspects as well as speak with the families and friends of the missing person.

Education:
Missing persons investigators can be either private detectives or they can work with a police force. The first step in either case is a high school diploma. A bachelor's degree in criminal justice or a related field is recommended, and it is required if the person wants to work for the Federal Bureau of Investigation (FBI). A private investigator must complete training and paperwork to carry a weapon; this training is standard in the police force. Anyone who wants to work with the police must go through police training and work their way up to detective over several years, gaining experience along the way. A minimum of three years' experience is required to be an FBI agent or private investigator. A private investigator's experience may include law enforcement work or working with a private investigation company. Both public and private detectives must also receive training related directly to missing persons cases, including the technology and procedures that are used.

Qualifications:
People who want to become missing persons investigators must have patience, enjoy figuring out mysteries, have good social skills, and work well in high-stress environments. They must also be able to handle disappointment, since not all cases end happily.

Salary:
$44,500 to $80,000 per year (a private detective generally earns less than a police detective)

beautiful prom dress and she had to sit on the sidelines."[47]

Other factors also pointed to Young's involvement, such as a series of text messages between him and Abbi in the hours before she ran away. However, when police interviewed Young, he denied knowing anything about Abbi's whereabouts. He also refused to take a polygraph (lie detector) test, which made police question whether he was telling the truth. However, when police searched his apartment, they found no evidence of his involvement in Abbi's disappearance.

After almost three weeks, a caller who wished to remain anonymous advised police to search the attic of the building Young lived in—directly above Young's apartment. After getting a warrant, investigators were met by Young, who angrily insisted that Abbi was not there.

The police continued to search, and they found her huddled in the attic, hiding in the insulation. Because he lied to the officers, Young was arrested for interfering with a police investigation.

Sometimes Tips Are Not Enough

Although a tip or a lead from a friend or finding a bit of information in the runaway's belongings is helpful, it does not guarantee that the runaway will be found.

One night in July 2014, when Megan Nichols, a 15-year-old from Fairfield, Illinois, said she was not feeling well and wanted to go to bed, her mother Kathy Jo Hutchcraft agreed to let her stay home by herself. It was not until later, when Kathy Jo went to check in on Megan, that she realized something was very wrong: Megan was gone. Unfortunately, when Kathy Jo went to the police, no immediate actions were taken.

Upon further inspection of Megan's room, Kathy Jo found her daughter's cell phone, but all the data had been wiped clean from it. She also found a note from Megan, in which the teen had revealed that she was never going to be happy where she was. A friend told Kathy Jo to check the bank accounts, and sure enough, money had been withdrawn. Bank footage showed Megan on the day of her disappearance, withdrawing funds on her bike.

When Kathy Jo gave the note and the wiped phone to the police, an investigation began. The investigators followed a few leads. One of the most promising leads was that Megan had been involved in a love triangle. According to Kathy Jo, the young man was 18 and seeing another girl. Kathy Jo had put a stop to the relationship, but it had carried on secretly, all the way up until Megan's disappearance. According to phone records, Megan had made phone calls to the young man on the day she went missing. The police have stated he is not a suspect in the investigation.

In this case, the presence of good leads—the bank and cell phone records—was not enough. As of September 2017, Megan had still not been located.

There Is Hope

Working on runaway cases can be

emotionally draining for police officers. Stark, who has worked many such cases, says that seeing the anger and unhappiness within families is often wrenching: "You feel bad for the family, bad for the kids who can't work through the stuff that's going on. You wish you could, you know, wave a wand or something, and have everybody just listen to one another."[48]

The best part of the job, he said, is seeing a teenager who has had problems in the past put the unhappiness and anger behind them: "I remember there was this one kid ... He was ... having a terrible time in his family, lots of bad stuff going on. But he got himself cleaned up, walks up to me at his school, and I was amazed to see that he was way better than before."[49] Stark said he did not know what had changed, but seeing an at-risk teen find a better life gave him hope for others in that position.

Chapter Three
Taken

When a child or adult goes missing and it is suspected that they have been abducted, the situation becomes especially frightening. Kidnappings can be difficult to solve, particularly when the perpetrator is not connected to the victim. An example of a connection is a parent who has taken their child without permission from the parent who has custody, or parental responsibility. According to the National Center for Missing & Exploited Children, 203,000 children are kidnapped by a family member each year, while about 58,200 children are abducted by non-family members. "These are young people who are taken against their will by a stranger or an acquaintance who has absolutely no business doing so, and very often these children are sexually assaulted, or physically harmed in other ways,"[50] Rivera said.

Police say that while all criminal investigations are important, non-family abductions are extremely urgent. While finding and arresting the abductor is important, finding the victim is crucial—hopefully before they are assaulted or killed. "There's no other way to say it," Stark said. "You're really racing the clock on cases like these. The urgency is very real—we've got statistics that say that when an abducted child turns up dead, most of the time it happens within three hours of the abduction."[51]

The Abduction of Amber Hagerman

The kidnapping of nine-year-old Amber Hagerman in Arlington, Texas, is an example of a case that could not be solved in time. On January 13, 1996, Amber and her younger brother were practicing riding their bikes in the parking lot of an abandoned grocery store near their grandparents' house. Neighbor Jim Kevil heard a scream and saw a man drag Amber into a black pickup truck, then speed away.

Kevil could give only a vague description of the truck and driver, but the Arlington police began searching right away. The FBI got involved, too, but without success. Four days later, an apartment security guard found Amber's body in a creek with her throat cut.

The town was devastated at the loss of the little girl. Her grandmother, Glenda Whitson, said that she was struck by how quickly their world had been turned around. From the time Amber began her bike ride to the moment Kevil made the 911 call to the police, less than 10 minutes had gone by. "People have to know that this is how fast these things can happen,"[52] she said.

By the Numbers

8,000

approximate number of leads received by police in the Amber Hagerman case

The Making of AMBER Alert

Police worked on Amber's case for more than 18 months, following thousands of leads. Even with the offer of a $75,000 reward, they had no luck finding the man who had abducted Amber. He seemed, some said, to have simply disappeared into thin air.

However, while the case had not been resolved, something positive had resulted from it—an idea proposed by a Dallas man who had followed the case carefully. Calling in to a local radio station, the man wondered about setting up a media system that would inform the public immediately when such a crime occurred. Just as radio and television stations transmit information during a severe weather alert, they could transmit a description of the child, the abductor, and the vehicle so the public could be on the lookout.

The idea was a good one, and in 1996, the Dallas–Fort Worth area adopted what became known as the AMBER Alert. "AMBER" is named for Amber Hagerman, and the letters also stand for "America's Missing: Broadcast Emergency Response." Today all 50 states have adopted the AMBER system, and it has been credited with helping to find hundreds of abducted children. The AMBER alert system was unified in 2003 into a national system, and according to the U.S. Department of Justice, as of 2014, it had helped save the lives of 711 children nationwide.

When AMBER Alerts Are Effective

The AMBER Alert is not activated for

More than 20 years after Amber's abduction, the killer has yet to be found.

every missing child. Police and other experts feel it is only effective when it is used for high-risk situations in which a child is in danger. If it were used for runaways or other cases with no immediate threat, the system would be used too often, and the public would be less likely to pay attention to the alerts.

"We had a case awhile back where the parents were divorced, and they shared custody of their two kids—a boy and girl, ages eight and six," said Wallace, a retired police officer.

The wife is mad at the husband, and decides to take the kids to a movie or something, even though it wasn't her day to be with them. So he calls us, and reports them missing. But no, we couldn't do the AMBER Alert, because there was absolutely no reason to suspect those kids were in any danger at all. The husband was [angry] because he thought the AMBER alert was [automatically sent], but this is exactly why it isn't.[53]

Police say that when it is used correctly, the AMBER Alert system is an amazing tool. One case that demonstrates this was the abduction in November 2009 of a two-year-old from Sanford, Maine. The parents were divorced, and the mother had custody. The father, who had severe anger issues, broke into the home and assaulted his ex-wife at knifepoint. He then took the little girl and left. The girl's mother quickly called police. Believing the little girl was in danger, they issued an AMBER Alert with a description of the child, the father, and the truck.

A hunter in New Hampshire heard the alert on the radio and memorized the information. Not long afterward, while driving on an unpaved road in the woods, the hunter came across the father and daughter in the vehicle described in the AMBER Alert. The hunter and the man talked for about an hour, then went to a nearby house, where police were called and the girl was released safely.

Eyewitness Memory

Police detectives are aware of the difficulties witnesses have in accurately describing a vehicle or a person who might be of interest in a criminal case. Someone who was in the area when a child was abducted, for example, might have seen the car but is unable to recall details about it—what kind of car it was, if it was damaged in some way, whether it seemed like a new car, or what letters and numbers were on the license plate.

Hannah McGill, a Minneapolis woman, once witnessed a car running a stop sign, severely injuring a mother riding her bicycle with her child seated on the back. She explained why recalling a high-risk situation can be difficult:

AMBER Alert messages can be used to alert the public to keep an eye out for cars that may be involved in a suspected kidnapping. Law enforcement officials prefer to use the AMBER Alert only in high-risk situations.

Things happen so quickly. You are looking; you're seeing what is happening, and you're caught up in the horror of what's happening. It's not like a movie, or a TV show. Like with me, I saw the car, but really didn't see it, you know? You want to be able to give [police] the year, make, model, color, but all you can say is, "It was gray … I think."[54]

Sometimes multiple witnesses remember different details. In fact, memories are not constant but changeable. Each time an event is remembered, the mind fills in the details and often invents little bits. The more a person recalls an event, the further the memory of the event is from the actual truth of what happened. In police investigations, witnesses may be affected by something they have seen or heard. This is called the misinformation effect. For example, if someone witnesses a man with blonde hair come into the room but is later asked about a man with brown hair, their memory may be altered to the point where they actually remember seeing a man with brown hair. Because of the misinformation effect, police have to be extra careful in the questioning of eyewitnesses.

By the Numbers

40

percentage of
stranger-abducted
children who are killed

An Unlikely Description

The difficulty of providing an accurate account of a stressful situation is why police were surprised when a teenage boy came forward in January 2007 with a detailed description of a vehicle believed to be involved in a recent child abduction. As it turned out, the description was the key to breaking not one but two abduction cases.

As it did every afternoon, the school bus dropped 13-year-old Ben Ownby off at his stop, just a few feet from his front door in the town of Beaufort, Missouri. However, he never arrived home, and as the hours went by without word, his parents became very worried.

A neighbor, 15-year-old Mitch Hults, verified that Ben got off the bus but added that he saw something at the time that surprised him. He told Ben's father, Don Ownby, that he saw a strange pick-up truck accelerate very quickly close to where Ben got off the bus. That is when Ownby realized that the disappearance of his son might be something very sinister and he needed to contact the police.

Franklin County sheriff Gary Toelke alerted the FBI. Agents immediately brought Mitch in for questioning and were astonished at the accuracy of his description of the truck. Not only did he remember the make, model, and color of the car, he remembered tiny details such as the fact that it had a two-inch trailer hitch on the back and rust or dirt over the fender. Toelke later said, "He was so accurate in what he told us, we kind of wondered if he made it up ... So we interviewed him until about 2 in the morning."[55]

The only thing Hults's description lacked was the license plate number of the truck. Even without that, an AMBER Alert was immediately issued for Ben, complete with the detailed description of the suspicious truck. In the meantime, forensic technicians made a plaster cast of the tread mark left on the dirt road near the bus stop where Ben was abducted. A tread mark for a vehicle is like a person's fingerprint. By examining the tread mark, experts can determine not only the make, size, and style of tire, they can also see little flaws or spots that show wear and tear that are unique to that particular tire. Hopefully, investigators thought, it would come in handy if they were to locate a suspect's vehicle.

A Surprise Break

Investigators did not have to wait long for a response. The description of the white truck caught the eye of Mike Prosperi, who ran a pizza shop in nearby Kirkwood, Missouri, only a 45-minute drive from Beaufort. Prosperi employed a manager, 41-year-old Mike Devlin, who owned a truck that fit the AMBER Alert description.

Prosperi had noticed Devlin acting oddly the day before and remembered that Devlin had asked to go home early because he did not feel well. Prosperi decided to drive by Devlin's apartment, where he noticed something suspicious. "I noticed that there was the red road dust like that you can get from driving on a gravel road out in the country," Prosperi recalled. "If he was ill ... I was wondering how he would have gotten that road dust."[56]

The next two days, Devlin called in sick, and Prosperi decided to call police. He told them Devlin had left at 12:50 p.m. on the day Ben Ownby was abducted. The FBI came out the following day to investigate. Agent Lynn Willett began to ask Devlin questions, and she noticed right away that he was displaying a lot of guilty body language; for instance, he looked down and did not meet her eyes.

Finally, she told him that they had a tire tread mark from the scene and explained that if it matched a tire on his truck, it would point to his guilt as much as a fingerprint would. With that, Devlin admitted to the kidnapping, and when he led officers to his home, they found not only Ben but also an older boy. That boy turned out to be Shawn Hornbeck, who had been abducted more than four years before.

Old Cases and New Media

On Saturday, October 22, 2005, Georgia teacher and former beauty queen Tara Grinstead attended a beauty pageant, then spent a few hours in the evening at a friend's barbecue just a few blocks from her house. She left the party around 11 p.m. and went straight home.

When Tara did not show up for work on Monday morning, the students became concerned and informed the faculty, who then telephoned the police. When they arrived at Tara's home, her unlocked car was in the driveway

A Cold Case

Police are extremely frustrated when a missing child case goes unsolved. Sometimes it can take years for a breakthrough that leads to answers.

Once such case was Etan Patz, a six-year-old who disappeared in 1979 on the way to his school bus stop. On May 25, his mother allowed him to walk two blocks to the bus stop alone for the first time. She was very worried when he did not come home on the bus after school, and she became frantic when she learned he had never arrived. Though hundreds of police officers combed New York's SoHo neighborhood looking for clues to Etan's whereabouts, no sign of the boy was found, and after weeks of searching, the case turned cold.

It was not until 2012 that the brother-in-law of Pedro Hernandez, a former bodega stock clerk, called authorities to voice his suspicions that Hernandez might have been involved. Almost 33 years after Etan Patz had vanished, Hernandez confessed to killing the boy. On February 14, 2017, Hernandez was found guilty and later sentenced to 25 years to life in prison. It had taken almost 38 years for the Patz family to see some kind of resolution.

STILL MISSING

POLICE DEPARTMENT
CITY OF NEW YORK

LOST CHILD ETAN PATZ

Missing Since Friday May 25th, 1979. Last seen 8 a.m., at Prince St. & West B'way.

DESCRIPTION:
Date of Birth: October 9, 1972   Male, White, 6 yrs.
Height: 40 Inches   Weight: 50 lbs.
Blond Hair, Blue Eyes, Wearing Black Pilot Type Cap, Blue Corduroy Jacket, Blue Pants, Blue Sneakers with Fluorescent Stripes; Carrying Blue Cloth Bag with Elephants Imprinted.
Persons Having Any Information Are Requested To Call
(212) 374-6913

After six-year-old Etan Patz's disappearance in 1979, a nationwide campaign to find him was launched. His photo was the first to appear on milk cartons that circulated the nation. The case did not close until 2017.

and the front door was locked. Using a neighbor's key, investigators entered and discovered an almost normal home. However, there were a few abnormalities: The lampshade was tilted in an odd position, the alarm clock was on the floor, a broken necklace lay on the floor, and Tara's cell phone was sitting neatly in its charger. Her purse and car keys were gone.

Tara was gone without a trace. Her family and the police suspected right from the beginning that something violent had happened to her. Investigators continued to look for Tara's remains while they questioned more than 100 people who had known Tara. However, there were no answers for more than 10 years, and it become the largest case file—the case with the largest amount of documentation—in Georgia.

Payne Lindsey, a film industry professional, was looking for a cold case in 2015 to create a documentary. On the Georgia Bureau of Investigation's (GBI) online cold case files, he came across the story of Tara Grinstead. He made a few phone calls to find out more about the case. Before he knew it, he was involved.

Lindsey created the real-time podcast *Up and Vanished* to document his research into the Grinstead case. Nearly every week, he reported on the findings of his legwork. He conducted multiple interviews with the townspeople of Ocilla, where Grinstead lived, as well as forensic and law specialists.

Then, on February 23, 2017, the GBI held a press conference where they announced the arrest of Ryan Duke, who had been a student at Ocilla's Irwin County High school, where Grinstead had been a teacher. What surprised everyone was that Ryan had never come up during the course of the investigation. Bo Dukes, another student who had been friends with Ryan at the time of Grinstead's murder, was also arrested on charges of concealing death and tampering with evidence. At the press conference, the GBI thanked the media for playing an important role in the investigation.

An interview with the news program *48 Hours* later surfaced with Bo's ex-girlfriend, Brooke Sheridan, who claimed to give vital information to the GBI after Bo told her about the murder. On an episode of *Up and Vanished*, she revealed what Bo had supposedly told her—that Ryan had broken into Grinstead's home and murdered her, and that afterward he had convinced Bo to help dispose of her body. The two of them had burned her body in a bonfire in a pecan orchard that was owned by Bo's relatives.

In July 2017, Bo pleaded not guilty, and the case went to trial. However, in September 2017, new charges were brought against Bo when it was discovered that he had lied to the GBI. He stated that he did not know anything about Grinstead's death when in fact

Ryan had confessed the whole thing to him. He also denied discussing it with anyone else, but police believe he did discuss it with a man named John McCullough. No further information about McCullough's connection to the case has been released.

Information after the arrest has been difficult to come by. The judge issued a gag order, which is a rule that the case is not to be discussed in public under penalty of law. This kind of protective order is used to protect the rights of individuals involved in the case. Sometimes high profile cases can be swayed by public opinion, thus denying a defendant's right to a fair trial. In the case of Bo, the judge's order only restricted family, potential witnesses, police, and court officials from speaking about the case. The judge has the difficult job of weighing the right of the public to an open court proceeding and the rights of the defendant.

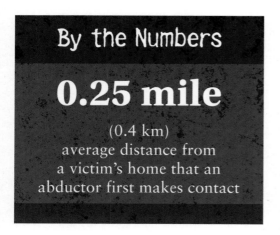

By the Numbers

0.25 mile

(0.4 km)
average distance from
a victim's home that an
abductor first makes contact

The Role of Social Media

While *Up and Vanished* did not solve the Grinstead case, it had another very important role—it pushed the details that were known into the public eye. Many people believe that by keeping the case relevant, the podcast got people talking and maybe brought new information to light.

Social media has become a very important tool in finding new details. Information spreads like wildfire. Before the Internet, missing children's photographs were distributed on milk cartons or hung on telephone poles. Posting a photo or description on the Internet is like posting millions of fliers on telephone poles. For example, when a two-year-old girl's body washed ashore in a trash bag on Deer Island in Winthrop, Massachusetts, in 2015, police were unable to identify her. She was given the name "Baby Doe," and a composite image was created and posted on social media. Within two weeks of posting that image online, an estimated 47 million people had seen it on Facebook.

A tip that came in due to this media campaign confirmed that "Baby Doe" was Bella Bond. The resulting investigation saw Bella's mother Rachelle Bond and her boyfriend Michael McCarthy, both heroin addicts, arrested. McCarthy was sentenced to life in prison with parole eligibility in 20 years for second-degree murder.

A memorial to Bella Bond, or "Baby Doe," formed at the site where her body was found. A photo of her is in the center of the memorial.

Michael McCarthy (far left) was found guilty of murdering "Baby Doe," later discovered to be two-year-old Bella Bond, the daugher of Rachelle Bond (far right).

Rachelle pleaded guilty to being an accessory to murder because she helped McCarthy dispose of the body. She served less than two years in jail; in July 2017, she was released and sent to a substance abuse rehabilitation center.

However, some people believe social media can sometimes do more harm than good. For example, when a person has been kidnapped and is still alive, a very public social media campaign could encourage the kidnapper to kill the victim as a way of covering their tracks. A social media campaign may also generate a lot of tips that are incorrect, sending the investigators in the wrong direction. This could waste precious time and resources. Additionally, using social media may worry some people. For example, in 2017, police in Washington, D.C., started sharing missing persons information on Twitter. This made many people believe the number of missing persons cases had increased. In reality, it had decreased; people just thought it had increased because they were hearing about it more often. It is important for police investigators to use social media in a responsible way, especially when it comes to time-sensitive cases.

Chapter Four
No Body?

When a missing person has been gone for a long time, in most cases the investigators believe that person to be dead. The case turns from a "rescue" status to "recovery," as with the Tara Grinstead case. However, even if law enforcement knows who is responsible, it can be very difficult to prosecute without a key piece of evidence: the victim's body.

"The Body of Crime"

The reason for this difficulty is actually an important principle in the legal systems of the United States, Canada, and many European countries. Known as *corpus delicti*, Latin for "the body of crime," it means a person cannot be convicted for a particular crime without evidence that that crime was actually committed in the first place.

For example, to try a person for committing arson—deliberately setting fires to destroy buildings—evidence of corpus delicti would be the burned property. To try someone for murder, evidence of corpus delicti is almost always a dead body. The reason such evidence is necessary, of course, is to avoid a situation in which a suspect is convicted and imprisoned (and in some cases, executed) for a serious crime such as murder, only to have the supposed victim show up later, unharmed.

The body of a murder victim is not absolutely necessary, as long as other strong, compelling evidence indicates that a murder occurred. However, that can be difficult to prove, and if prosecutors fail to persuade the jury, they can never try the suspect again—even if they later do find the body. "It's called double jeopardy," explained Minnesota attorney Paul J. Zech. "It's another principle of the legal system, that you can't be tried twice for the same crime. So yes, there are times when the state does go ahead and prosecute even though they have no body, but it is risky."[57]

Not surprisingly, then, many

abductors make an effort to dispose of the body of a victim so carefully that it will never be found. Over the years, abductors have buried victims in remote locations, burned bodies, dismembered them (cut them apart), and thrown them in shark-infested waters and crocodile-filled swamps. In spite of such actions on the part of the abductor, however, police are often able to locate the body—or parts of it—to make a positive identification. Fortunately, sometimes only a very small piece of a body is needed to convict someone. If law enforcement officials find a piece of bone that tests positive for the DNA of the missing person, for instance, this is proof that the missing person is no longer alive. However, such evidence is not foolproof. The duty of a defendant's lawyer is to prove that the defendant had nothing to do with the crime. For this reason, even if a body is found, they may argue that just because the missing person is dead, it does not prove a murder was committed. Other evidence is necessary to prove to a jury beyond a reasonable doubt that the person on trial actually did murder someone.

The Acid Bath Murderer

John George Haigh, an Englishman who murdered at least six people between 1944 and 1949, did not completely understand the idea of corpus delicti. He was certain the Latin phrase referred to

Serial killer John George Haigh is shown in this photograph from 1949.

Even though they did not find a body, police found enough evidence by searching John George Haigh's property (shown here) to charge him with murder.

an actual corpse, so he assumed he could not be convicted if police could not find the bodies of his victims. To make certain no one could find the bodies after he shot them, he put them in large drums of sulfuric acid. The acid turned the bodies into sludge, which he then poured into the sewers.

When Haigh's hotel room and workshop were searched after the disappearance of his final victim, a wealthy 69-year-old woman named Olivia Durand-Deacon, the police found a dry-cleaning receipt for a woman's fur coat, a glass container called a carboy, a steel drum, a pump, and a revolver. When questioned by the police, Haigh reportedly said, "Mrs. Durand-Deacon no longer exists. She has disappeared completely and no trace of her will ever be found again."[58]

Haigh's workshop was searched a second time, and this time investigators found blood stains and a puddle of sludge on the side of the building. Dr. Keith Simpson, a Scotland Yard pathologist, sieved the soil around the sludge and uncovered 28 pounds (12.7 kg) of human body fat, part of a left foot, bone fragments, three human gallstones—fluid that hardens in the gallbladder, causing stomach pain—a complete set of dentures, and the handle of a red purse. A dental surgeon was consulted, and it was confirmed that the dentures were custom-fitted to Durand-Deacon's mouth. All this evidence was enough: The court charged Haigh with Durand-Deacon's murder on March 2, 1949.

Since Haigh's time, there have been many attempts to get rid of evidence using acid. However, scientists have developed methods to expose the perpetrators. For example, when Erwin Vermeij at the Netherlands Forensic Institute received "a large, moist, off-white block"[59] from the garden of a suspected drug trafficker, he looked at it under a microscope. He explained what he saw:

> I noticed unusual pink and brown dots. Under the microscope, they were made up of sand and strange, irregularly shaped, thin-walled structures, which turned out to contain calcium, phosphorous and fluorine. When we find calcium and phosphorous in a forensic investigation, alarm bells start ringing because bone contains these minerals.[60]

After further research and experiments, Vermeij was able to determine that the body of the victim had been cremated, or burned, to destroy protein, fat, and bone structure. Then it was soaked in acid and disposed of. Using this research, the court convicted the suspect, who was sentenced to 18 years in jail.

Determining the Crime Scene

One important start to solving any abduction case in which murder is suspected is to find and process the crime scene. Often, "crime scene" refers to the location where the crime occurred, but it can also be any place where activities related to that crime occurred. The very nature of an abduction almost always means the discovery of multiple crime scenes that could give clues— the place where the abduction occurred, the spot where the

In the case of an abduction, police often collect evidence from multiple crime scenes.

NO NOT CROSS   SHERIFF'S LINE DO NOT CROSS   SHERIFF'S LINE DO NOT CROSS

Occupation: Crime Scene Investigator

Job Description:
Crime scene investigators (CSIs) examine a crime scene for evidence, such as hairs, fingerprints, or the presence of hidden blood. They collect this evidence and bring it to a forensics lab for analysis. They also take photographs of the crime scene and note anything that seems unusual.

Education:
The type of education needed depends on the place that is offering the job. Some positions require only a high school diploma, but most require a bachelor's of science (BS) degree in forensic science, forensic anthropology, biology, or chemistry. People who do not have a BS in forensic science may be required to take additional courses to earn what is called a certificate. Certificate courses teach people about a specific topic but take less time to complete than a degree.

Qualifications:
Being a CSI requires extreme attention to detail; they must be able to spot small items such as hairs and figure out which parts of a crime scene are the most important—something that is not always obvious. They must also have strong problem-solving and organizational skills, and they must not be bothered by blood, dead bodies, and other graphic scenes.

Salary:
$34,000 to $94,400 per year

victim was taken, the vehicle used to transport the victim, the place where the victim's body was hidden or disposed of, and so on.

However, finding a crime scene can be very complicated. In fact, some are actually invisible. In her book *Every Contact Leaves a Trace*, Connie Fletcher interviewed a forensic technician who worked a missing persons case in Maryland. A young woman had mysteriously vanished, which alarmed most of her family, though it did not seem to worry her husband. At first, when her family members would call, the husband would tell them she was out doing errands or visiting friends. However, as the days went by, the woman's family became very worried and called the police to report her missing.

Suspicion quickly fell upon the husband because he had made several large withdrawals from his wife's bank account—to pay large gambling debts, as it turned out. However, though police searched the home for signs of a body, they found nothing at all unusual. They looked in the yard, too, for some indication that he might have buried her. However, they found no trace of her, and investigators were confused.

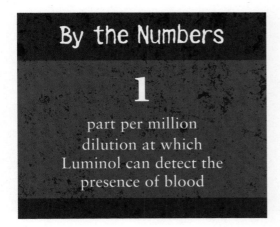

By the Numbers

1

part per million dilution at which Luminol can detect the presence of blood

Revealing Hidden Blood

Sometimes the mark of a wise detective is to know not only which questions to ask but to whom those questions should be addressed. Somewhere, the detectives believed, there was a crime scene, and it would give them some forensic evidence that would help them find the wife's body and determine the cause of her death. In this case, recalled the forensic specialist, since the husband was little help, detectives asked her family members to come to the house to see if anything looked different to them. They noticed that a sleeper sofa in the basement was no longer there. This was significant to detectives because in the summer, the wife "would routinely go downstairs. And she'd lie on the sleeper sofa, watch TV, do whatever, and sometimes even sleep down there if the evenings were really hot. And that sofa was missing."[61]

Investigators suspected that the sofa had been a crime scene and that the husband had quickly gotten rid of it. No sign of blood was found in the empty space, on the nearby wall, or anywhere else.

However, forensic specialists have a tool that can make even cleaned-up blood visible. It is a chemical agent known as Luminol that technicians mix with other chemicals, such as hydrogen peroxide, and spray on surfaces they suspect might have had blood on them. Even if the blood has been cleaned up carefully with soap and hot water, traces of the hemoglobin (an iron-carrying protein within a red blood cell) will still be present. The iron within the

Luminol and ultraviolet light reveal traces of blood that cannot be detected by the human eye.

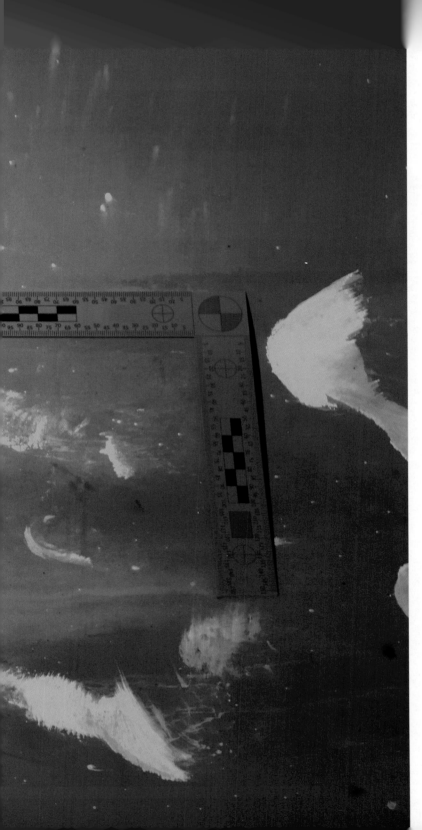

hemoglobin will react with the Luminol mixture and create a whitish-blue glow when the room is darkened.

Crime Scene Found

In the case of the Maryland woman, the forensic technician recalled how quickly the theory of the missing sofa being a possible crime scene turned out to be a good one:

I applied Luminol to the area [where the sofa had been], sprayed it, and ... with the lights turned out, and with this chemical liquid sprayed all over everything, what showed up was luminescence of the wall outlining the back of the sofa, on the floor, outlining where the sofa would have been if it was pulled out, and then showing other luminescent marks going right into the bathroom in the basement.[62]

Finding this crime scene was a crucial bit of forensic work, and it opened up important new leads. After following the blood trail into the basement bathroom, forensic workers found traces of human tissue in the drain of the bathtub—and those led to a DNA match to the victim.

The Power of DNA

DNA, short for deoxyribonucleic acid, is the genetic material that is found in the nucleus of all cells of the body. Most of the pattern in the two long, entwined threads of DNA in a cell's nucleus is the same for all humans, but 0.1 percent of it is unique to each individual, except in the case of identical twins. That small part is what is used to tie DNA from the crime scene to an individual.

The case against the husband was further

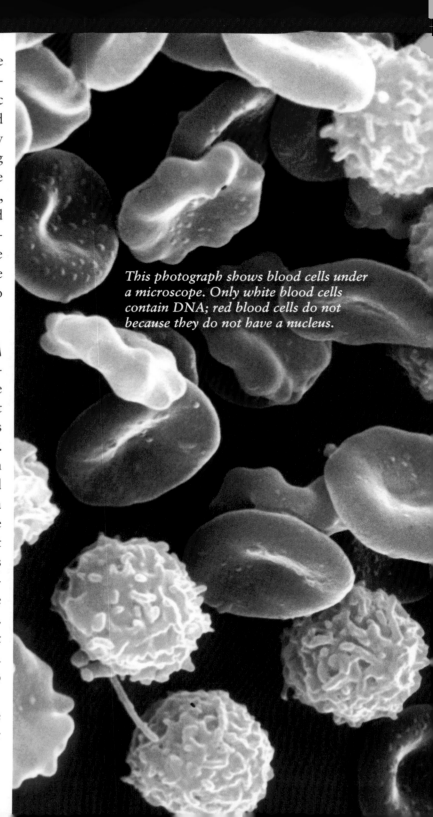

This photograph shows blood cells under a microscope. Only white blood cells contain DNA; red blood cells do not because they do not have a nucleus.

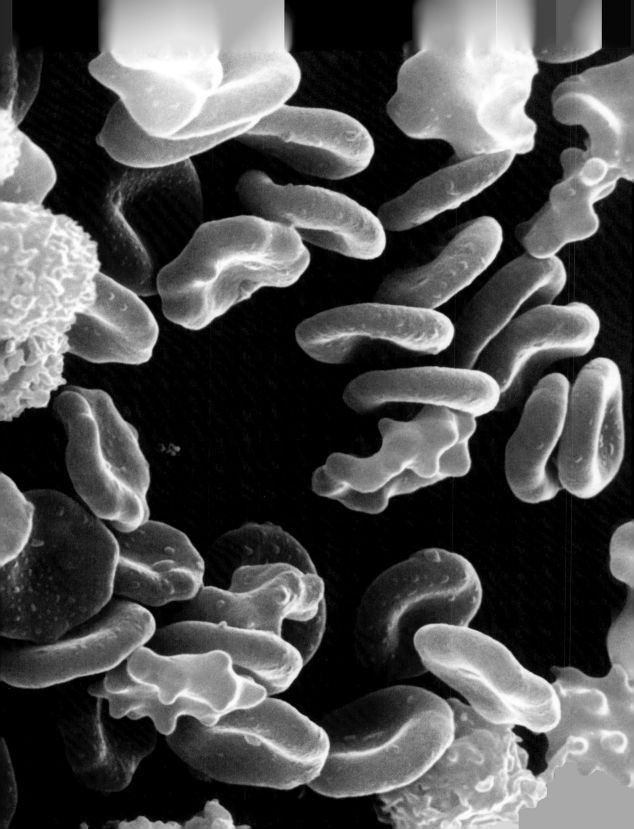

DNA Evidence and CODIS

DNA evidence has become an important tool in solving missing persons cases, but some people are unaware that it would not be nearly as helpful without a special database. It is called CODIS, which stands for Combined DNA Index System. CODIS enables law enforcement agencies to compare DNA evidence found at crime scenes with millions of samples collected from people who have been arrested for violent crimes. With a sample of DNA from semen, saliva, or blood, investigators from the United States can search for a match—and hopefully find the offender they are looking for.

However, there are limits to DNA technology, even with CODIS. For example, only people who have previously been convicted of a crime are entered into the database. This means a first-time offender may not be caught because the police will not have his or her DNA in CODIS yet. Additionally, DNA analysts sometimes make mistakes that cause them to match DNA at a crime scene to the wrong suspect. DNA analysis is an important tool that has caught many criminals, but it is important for people to remember that no technology is 100 percent foolproof.

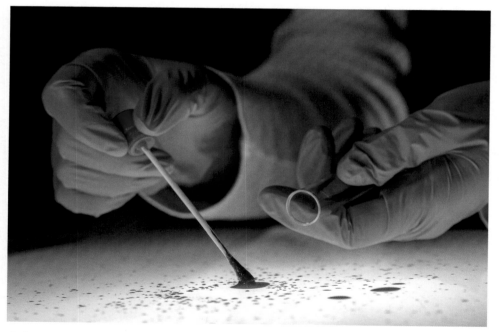

A forensic scientist can extract DNA from samples of blood and other bodily fluids found at a crime scene.

strengthened when detectives located a trash collector who had been contacted by the husband to haul the sofa to the dump. The trash collector said the sofa—which he said was in very good condition, unlike other furniture he had been paid to dump—was much heavier than it should have been.

"Of course, when the detectives went to the landfill—this was maybe a week after the event—there was no way they could find it,"[63] the forensic specialist told Fletcher. However, in this case, even without a body, the discovery of the crime scene and the leads it provided was enough to convict the husband of murder.

Bodies in Water

In some cases, the abductor disposes of the body in water—something that presents its own complex set of challenges for investigators. Sometimes diving teams are sent out to search if they have some idea of the area where a body might have been dumped. In many cases, a victim's body surfaces and washes ashore on its own—sometimes bringing evidence that can catch a murderer.

This happened in October 2001 when a man's body washed ashore in New Melones Reservoir, a man-made lake in Calaveras County, California. Even a quick look showed

detectives that this was no drowning victim. The man's hands had been tied behind his back, and a hood covered his head. The body was identified as that of missing 58-year-old real estate developer Meyer Muscatel, a Russian immigrant who had been reported missing by his family not long before.

Police suspected that Muscatel was only one of several wealthy Russian immigrants who had recently been targeted by a group of eastern European kidnappers. These men lured their victims by arranging business meetings with them and then abducting them. The kidnappers contacted the families to demand ransom, threatening to kill the victims unless the money was paid. As the discovery of Muscatel revealed, however, the kidnappers had no intention of releasing their victims.

Using Side-Scan Sonar

Two people—including the girlfriend of one of the suspected kidnappers—supplied information about the crimes to detectives and agreed to testify against two of the suspects. However, detectives knew that to convict them of murder, finding any other bodies the suspects might have dumped in the same lake could be important. However, the lake was large and deep, and they would need an army of divers to search it all—

Greater than usual care must be taken to preserve evidence when a body is found underwater.

and even then, success would not be guaranteed.

Instead, they used a device called side-scan sonar, an instrument made for searching in very deep water. It has been used by the U.S. Navy to detect mines on the ocean bottom and by archaeologists to find shipwrecks. In recent years, it has also been a valuable tool in locating bodies.

The instrument consists of a torpedo-shaped device—about 4 feet (1.2 m) long—that is dragged behind a boat. It uses sound waves, or impulses (also called "pings"), to detect objects underwater. The pings bounce off objects and feed the data into a computer on the boat. The computer then processes the sound waves into an image of the object.

In this case, four more bodies were located—two under one bridge in 350 feet (106.7 m) of water, and two under a different bridge in 250 feet (76.2 m) of water. Thanks in large part to the discovery of the bodies, a jury convicted the kidnappers of murder.

In recent years, crime investigators have used side-scan sonar to locate bodies in deep water.

The Case of Michele Wallace

Success in locating the body of a missing person is almost always due to the cooperation and teamwork of forensics and investigative diligence. Few missing persons investigations have demonstrated that any better than the case of Michele Wallace, who disappeared in August 1974. Michele was an avid photographer and experienced outdoorswoman, and after saying goodbye to her parents, she took off in her car—a red Mazda—for a short camping trip in the Rocky Mountains. She took her black German shepherd with her. According to her father, she was stronger and more capable than most: "She was a tough little cookie. She climbed mountains, jumped out of airplanes and roped cattle. If you knew a boy who did half of what she did you'd say, 'What a guy!'"[64]

However, when she did not return on the date she had promised her parents she would, they became worried. They notified police, who put out an emergency message to law enforcement, radio, and television stations all across Colorado. When her dog was found shot to death by a rancher for chasing his cattle, her parents were heartbroken; they knew Michele would never have let the dog out of her sight if she had still been alive.

Soon afterward, however, the police got a tip. A ranch hand named Chuck Matthews called the sheriff's department and told them that he had seen Michele, and like her parents, he worried that she was in trouble. Matthews related how he had given a ride to a drifter named Roy Melanson, and the two of them were sitting in the car drinking beer when a young woman with long black braids and a German shepherd walked by. They offered her a ride to her car, and she accepted. However, just as they got to her car, Matthews's car broke down.

By the Numbers

24

percent decrease in missing persons cases between 2004 and 2013

Going Cold

Matthews said something very odd happened soon afterward. Just after Michele drove the two men back to Gunnison, Colorado, Matthews got out and thanked her, but Melanson asked if she would mind driving him to his car. That was very strange, he told police, because he swore that

Melanson had told him that he had no vehicle. So why was he asking for a ride to a car that did not exist?

That information worried police, who put out a Be On the Lookout (BOLO) alert for Roy Melanson. The alert became even more urgent when they learned the suspect had already served time in prison for rape and was currently wanted in Texas for another sexual assault.

When police finally caught up to Melanson, he was driving Michele's Mazda. He told police that she had let him borrow the car and that he had dropped her off at a bar. Melanson also had a receipt showing that he had sold all of her camera equipment. Believing he had already killed the young woman, police arrested him. However, without any sign of her body, they did not want to take their one chance to charge him with murder when their case could fail in court. Colorado police shipped Melanson back to Texas, and the missing persons case went nowhere.

Five years later, a key piece of evidence surfaced. On a July morning in 1979, a hiker found a human scalp while walking along a logging road not far from Gunnison. What made the scalp even more startling was that its black hair was intact, neatly parted in the middle, and was still in two long braids. He brought it into town and gave it to the sheriff, who recognized that it might be Michele's. He sent it to a crime lab for analysis, but technicians were not able to tell much about the hair without a known specimen of Michele's hair. Police organized another search near where the hair was found, but they came up empty-handed. Most likely, an animal had carried the scalp away from the location of the murder. Police placed the scalp in the evidence room. Once more, the case had gone cold.

Looking for Michele

Twelve years later, Kathy Young, a new investigator in the Gunnison County sheriff's office, decided to look over some cold cases and was fascinated by the Michele Wallace case. She submitted the scalp to the crime lab again for analysis, this time including a hairbrush that had been found in the backpack recovered in Michele's car. Years ago, after Melanson had been caught in Michele's car, her belongings had been cataloged. However, when the scalp was found years later and sent to the forensics lab, no one had thought to submit the brush from the evidence room. This time, a combination of a known sample of her hair and modern DNA technology showed a definite match. However, the hair alone was not enough to guarantee a guilty verdict without more of the body. Because of the double jeopardy rule that states a person cannot be charged for the same crime twice, Young did not want to take a chance that Melanson would go free despite what she believed he had done to Michele years ago.

Young had heard of a nonprofit forensic group who specialized in finding hidden bodies. They used a wide array of methods—not only cutting-edge technology but also the services of a group of scientists whose experience with botany, geology, medicine, animal behavior, and anthropology would help interpret data.

Young asked the group, called NecroSearch, if they would be willing to help look for Michele's remains. After hearing the story of the young photographer's disappearance, they agreed. In late fall 1991, the NecroSearch team began organizing their search, and Jack Swanburg, the group's cofounder, was optimistic. "There was only one Sherlock Holmes," he said, "but if you put all of these heads together and look at the technology that's available, you've got a supersleuth that's going to be tough to beat."[65]

Found

NecroSearch's botanist Vicki Trammell came up with an amazing amount of information from examining the scalp. First, she noted that the dark hair had been bleached by the sun in places, so she knew that Michele's body had almost certainly been dumped, not buried. She examined the pine needles, grass, and other debris on the hair and was able to tell searchers where they should begin looking. The matter was from a type of tree that grows best in cool, damp weather, so Trammell advised them to start searching on the north-facing mountain slopes.

The results were astonishing. On the second day of the search, Cecilia Travis was heading down a slope when she spied what she believed was a large white mushroom. As she got closer, however, she realized that it was not a mushroom but a skull. "This is a heavily wooded area," she recalled later, "and a ray of light came through and hit that cranium and it had a gold [filling]."[66] She recalled that Michele's physical description included a lot of dental work, and she knew right away whose skull she had found.

She called out to her fellow searchers and they all came running. "I knew I had Michele," Travis said. "To myself I said, 'It's all right Michele, we know now.'"[67]

In the end, it was an analysis of pine needles that led investigators to the remains of Michele Wallace.

Conspiracy Theories

Some missing persons cases are so mysterious that people begin to suspect some kind of conspiracy. For example, famous pilot Amelia Earhart disappeared on a flight around the world in 1937. Her plane, which was a type called an Electra, lost radio contact somewhere over the Pacific Ocean, and she and her navigator, Fred Noonan, were never seen again. The plane's crash site was never found.

Some people believe the plane ran out of gas and crashed into the ocean; others believe Earhart and Noonan flew off course, landed on a small uninhabited island called Nikumaroro, and died there. This theory is popular because searches have uncovered several artifacts, including "a piece of Plexiglass that may have come from the Electra's window, a woman's shoe dating back to the 1930s, improvised tools, a woman's cosmetics jar from the 1930s and bones that appeared to be part of a human finger."[1] Additionally, in June 2017, four bone-sniffing dogs appeared to locate the spots where Earhart and Noonan may have died, although no remains aside from the finger bone have been found.

However, the lack of hard evidence has given rise to several conspiracy theories. Many of these center around the Japanese, since World War II broke out shortly after Earhart disappeared. For example, various people have claimed that Earhart was sent to spy on the Japanese and was captured after she crashed; that she crashed, was captured by the Japanese military, and died in one of their prisons; that she was captured and ended up helping the Japanese spread war propaganda on the radio; that she escaped the Japanese prison, moved to New Jersey, and became a banker; and that she survived and became a nurse on the island of Guadalcanal during World War II. In 2017, a photo was found that many claimed showed Earhart and Noonan waiting to board a ship in the Marshall Islands after their disappearance. However, the photo was discredited when Kota Yamano, a Japanese military history blogger, discovered that the photo had actually been published in 1935. Whether or not the picture is of Earhart and Noonan, it could not have been taken after they disappeared in 1937.

1. "Amelia Earhart," History.com, accessed September 14, 2017. www.history.com/topics/amelia-earhart.

Soon afterward, the searchers began finding bits and pieces of clothing that could be traced back to Michele—part of a bra, a zipper from some blue jeans, and buttons. They also found bones—40 in all, including 25 foot bones within a boot. All were found to belong to Michele, and like the scalp, they had likely been scattered by animals in the years since her body had been dumped.

The discovery sealed the fate of her abductor and murderer Roy Melanson. He was convicted of first-degree murder in 1993 and sentenced to life in prison.

Chapter Five
Starting with J. Doe

In many cases, the police start a missing persons investigation when they find an unidentified body, often referred to as a John Doe or a Jane Doe. This process is like working a case backward. Detectives hope to look at the evidence they find on and around the body to determine the cause of death and, hopefully, the identity of the individual. If the death is a homicide, the next step is to find out who was responsible. According to Stark,

The thing is that a person found dead, whether it's natural causes or it looks like it could be foul play, or suicide or whatever it is—that person maybe had been reported missing, but now no one knows who to notify. That's the most frustrating part. [It] doesn't matter if the person was homeless or mentally ill or a drug user or an alcohol abuser—you'd like to think someone somewhere would *want to know that the person died, you know? But it's not easy to get that identity.*[68]

From the Body

Even without a picture ID, the body itself can offer much information that can help investigators. First of all, the body is photographed with any clothing that is still intact, then again without the clothing. The body is weighed and measured, and the hair color is determined, with the medical examiner noting whether it has been artificially bleached or colored.

Forensic workers look for something in the body's appearance that would be unusual—from a birthmark or tattoo to an artificial limb. "Anything you could put on a flier or release to the newspapers," said retired police officer Wallace. "'White male in his 30s or 40s' doesn't help much. [It helps to have] something more unique that could catch

The body and crime scene
are photographed from
every angle as part of the
evidence-collecting process.

the attention of someone who might say, 'Hey, you know, I used to work with a guy that had a tattoo like that,' or whatever."[69]

Physical Characteristics

The medical examiner takes fingerprints from the body, and those fingerprints are run through the FBI's Integrated Automated Fingerprint Identification System (IAFIS). IAFIS includes not only fingerprints but also physical characteristics such as height, weight, and hair and eye color, as well as tattoos or scars. However, there are limitations; while IAFIS includes a great deal of data—66 million criminal sets of fingerprints—experts say that much of the time, their unknown victims will not be included.

"While there are millions of sets of prints on file, unless you have a criminal background or have served in the U.S. armed forces, your prints are not likely to be in the IAFIS database," said Dr. Michael McGee, a medical examiner in Ramsey County, Minnesota. "Dental records are much better—pretty much everybody goes to the dentist. And they keep careful records: the X-rays, the

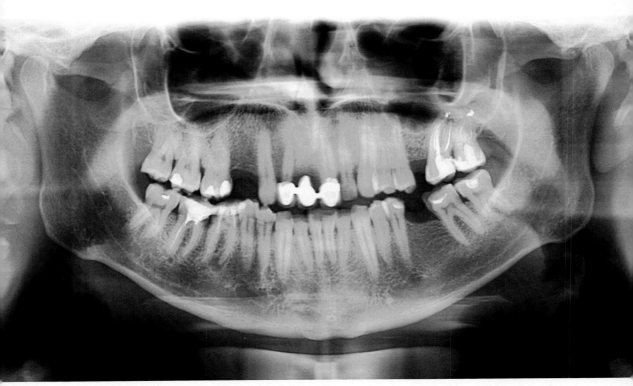

Dental records can be very helpful in discovering the identity of a John or Jane Doe.

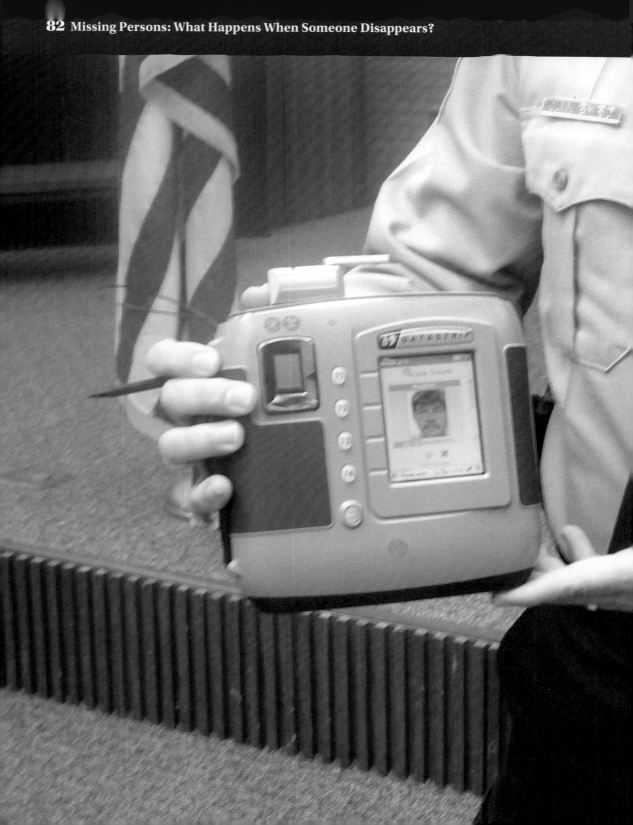

crowns, root canals, the pulled teeth. If we have a name or a possible identity for an unnamed victim, we will check dental records to see if there is a match."[70]

Once the external examination is done, the medical examiner does an autopsy, which can also provide clues to the identity of the body and provide more information about why the victim died. If the person had advanced cancer, severe arthritis, or only one kidney, that information could be included in a public description of the J. Doe. If the body has a pacemaker to help the heart work better, that can be another identifier. Devices such as that are numbered by the manufacturer and can be traced to a particular patient, giving an unidentified person back his or her name.

By the Numbers

162,000

number of fingerprints processed each day on IAFIS

The IAFIS is designed to be used by officers on the street and has the ability to record fingerprints and photos in the field while cross-checking the database.

Not Doing Enough

In some cases, identifying a John Doe or Jane Doe has been long delayed—even when a missing persons report has been filed. Many critics say this has occurred especially often in runaway cases, which in the past, some police departments have been less interested in solving. Studying such cases and how the system failed has helped departments make improvements in the way they operate.

This happened in the case of Michelle Vick, a 14-year-old Washington girl who ran away from home allegedly to be with her boyfriend. Her mother reported her missing right away, but the police did not follow up on the case. Police are supposed to obtain medical and dental records of a person missing longer than 30 days so they can be entered into the database. Vick's dental records were not submitted. Perhaps the police assumed that she, like many runaways, would come home.

Four months after she ran away, pheasant hunters were horrified to find the remains of what appeared to be a human body. It looked like someone might have tried to hide it, but coyotes or other small animals had scattered the remains.

Forensic workers did their job, noting not only the bullet holes in the skull but learning all they could about the victim from the remains. Three days after the body was discovered, they entered all the information into the computer database—the dental profile, estimated height and weight of the victim, and other details that could enable investigators to match the remains with a missing person. However, because police had not followed up on Vick's case, her records had never been entered into the computer.

Without that match between the missing persons report and the information from the medical examiner's office, police were not sure what to do. Jim Hansen, a Washington State homicide officer, remembered being shocked that they had found a murdered teenager who had not been reported missing. "Somebody knew this girl; somebody knew she was missing," he said. "It became a case of … 'why is this going on? How does something like this happen?'"[71]

The answer, it appeared, was because the system was not working. In fact, when the *Seattle Post-Intelligencer* did a story in 2003 on the failures of Washington's system of tracking the missing and identifying the dead, the reporters were stunned. In nearly two-thirds of missing persons cases, police had failed to do the required follow-up with dental records and medical histories. One of the reasons for the inadequate response may be that police became uninterested once they believed the person left voluntarily.

Vick's mother, Tish Curry, noted this attitude when she showed police the note Vick had left her, which talked about running away to be with her boyfriend. "After that, they just considered her a runaway, and no one looked for her. If she'd been 10 years old, they would have been frantically searching for her. Her face would've been all over TV."[72]

Vick's body was finally identified when a homicide detective in another part of the state noticed similarities between her death and the deaths of eight young prostitutes in Spokane—they all had been shot in the head and dumped in remote locations. When he requested dental records and found none, the detective checked on the computer list of missing girls and young women in that time period and saw Vick's name. Noting that her records were not on the computer, he called and got information about her. A forensic dentist compared the files he had with the chart made from the unidentified Jane Doe and got a match—almost a year and half after Vick's body was discovered.

Experts acknowledge that Vick's death would not have been prevented by dental records. Even so, those records would have given detectives a quicker start on a homicide investigation and, as reporter Lewis Kamb said, "they would have spared her family more than a year of anguish."[73]

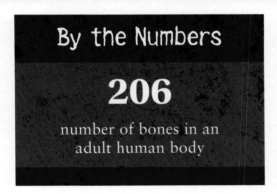

By the Numbers

206

number of bones in an adult human body

Facial Reconstruction: Bringing a Skull to Life

There are tools the police use that work extremely well. One of the most valuable tools, especially when a body is badly decomposed, is facial reconstruction. This is the process of taking a skull of a J. Doe and, by using a combination of art and science, creating a lifelike appearance that someone might recognize. Facial reconstruction is almost always done by a sculptor who has a background in facial anatomy. It can be used to help identify victims of crimes or mass disasters such as a plane crash or a terrorist attack.

Examination of the skull and other bones can provide information about the victim that can make important contributions to the reconstruction. The shape of a skull, for instance, can give experts an idea of the race of the victim. The skulls of people of African descent, for example, are more rounded, with wider spaces between the eye sockets, while the skulls of Caucasians are

Occupation: Forensic Anthropologist

Job Description:
Forensic anthropologists help identify unknown bodies or body parts and skeletal remains. They also help determine the estimated time since death and cause of death. Work is carried out both in the lab and in the field. The work involves exposure to potentially dangerous and disturbing situations.

Education:
Aspiring forensic anthropologists must first earn either a bachelor of arts degree (BA) or a bachelor of science degree (BS) in anthropology from a four-year college. According to Binghamton University in New York State, a BS degree focuses more on the science that is relevant to a career in forensics. After getting a bachelor's degree, the student can then get a master of arts (MA) degree in anthropology, a doctor of philosophy (PhD) degree in anthropology, or both. To be accepted into the PhD program at the University of Tennessee, Knoxville—the most respected forensic anthropology PhD program—an applicant must have either a BA or MA in anthropology or a minor in anthropology and a BS in a field such as biology or history. Other programs may have different requirements. Once their education is completed, forensic anthropologists may apply for board certification by the American Board of Forensic Anthropology.

Qualifications:
Aspiring forensic anthropologists must be objective, persistent, and enjoy solving puzzles. They must be able to handle situations involving death and decay.

Salary:
$31,000 to $89,000 per year

longer and have eye sockets closer together. Skulls of people of Asian descent have more prominent cheekbones, and the nasal opening is wide and flat.

Forensic anthropologists must estimate the size of the victim. Though the bones can easily show how tall the person was, they offer no good estimate of weight. "But you can tell from clothing," one forensic anthropologist told author Connie Fletcher. "Unless you have a homeless person and he picks up clothes out of a garbage can or the Salvation Army: he doesn't necessarily have clothes that fit him."[74] She said she

A forensic anthropologist uses knowledge of the human skeleton to assist with investigations.

looks for a belt, which would be fitted to the individual's comfort.

By identifying the sex, height, weight, and race of the victim, the reconstruction artist begins applying clay to "build" the face. This process is not just a matter of layering clay on the skull. Using tiny rubber or plastic pegs as markers—generally about 24 of them altogether—the artist glues them to various places on the skull. These pegs show the approximate thickness of flesh on various points of the face, based on the sex, age, and race of the victim, according to statistics kept by the FBI.

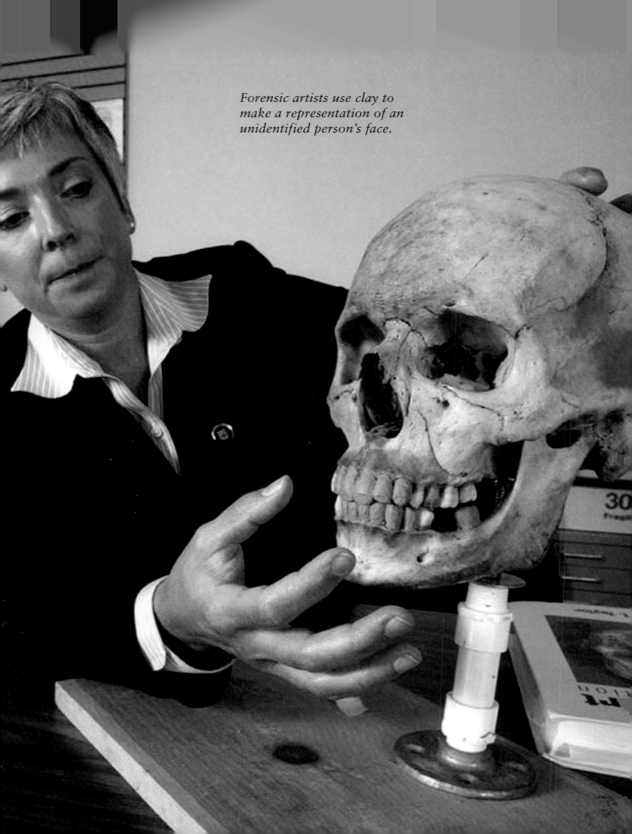

Forensic artists use clay to make a representation of an unidentified person's face.

When the sculpting phase is finished, hair and glass eyes are often added. When hair has been found on the remains, the artist supplies a wig to match. The reconstruction is not meant to be a perfect likeness—that would be impossible due to the limits of forensics. Even so, the reconstruction might be similar enough to remind someone who views it of the missing person.

The face, once completed, may be shown on television or on fliers that are posted in the area where the body was found. More and more, however, facial reconstructions are showing up on Internet websites. The NamUs is one of the most effective. Run by the U.S. Department of Justice, it contains more than 27,000 images of missing persons, as well as more than 14,000 unidentified remains or facial reconstructions.

NamUS is a free system that can be used by medical examiners, law enforcement, and the general public and has been praised by forensic workers and families of missing persons alike. Prior to NamUS, several other websites were operating with different databases, said Kevin Lothridge, CEO of the National Forensic Science Technology Center. He added, "Now there is one place where law enforcement and the public can look at the data. It's like having a million eyes looking at your case."[75]

The Case of Precious Doe

Sometimes, even with excellent facial reconstruction, a case may take years to be resolved. One of the most wrenching cases of unidentified victims was that of a little girl known as Precious Doe. On April 28, 2001, police in Kansas City, Missouri, were searching for an elderly man who had wandered away from his home when they came upon the decapitated (headless) body of a young African American girl. The body was unclothed, and no clues to her identity were found. Her head was discovered a few days later in a garbage bag—not far from where police found her body.

An autopsy showed that the little girl had been badly beaten before she died and that she was between three and six years old. Not surprisingly, the public was greatly outraged over the crime, as well as concerned that no one had reported her missing. Because she was so young, the police and community began referring to her as Precious Doe.

Her body was so badly decomposed that she could not be specifically described in a way that might ring true to someone who had known the child. Forensic artists did the best they could to reconstruct her face from the skull, but no tips came in. By December 2001, no one had come forward with any information about her, and the

Missing Clues

In some missing persons cases, investigators can get so focused on following one lead that they miss other important clues. In one case, a young woman named Megan disappeared for about two weeks because she had a mental breakdown. After suffering a PTSD flashback, Megan experienced a transient dissociative episode, which she described as follows:

> *It's a break that comes with amnesia, derealization, and depersonalization. Without warning I suddenly began thinking the band Snow Patrol were talking specifically to me [through the car radio]. The song was "Chasing Cars." They wanted me to chase cars? Drive! They wanted me to drive, but where? I grabbed a notebook and started writing because I had suddenly figured out how to solve world hunger. Then I realized where Snow Patrol wanted me to drive. The patent office! I had to get to the patent office so no one could steal my ideas!*[1]

No one was aware of Megan's mental state, so when her boyfriend called the police two days after she went missing, they assumed he had murdered her. By focusing on this lead rather than Megan's history of mental illness, they missed several chances to find her and return her to her home. In fact, she had three separate encounters with police officers while she was missing—none of whom recognized her. Additionally, many citizens do not see or pay attention to missing persons reports, so when she turned up at a nearby firehouse, the firemen there did not recognize her, either. She was sent to a mental health facility, which, she explained, made finding her next to impossible: "Unless an adult gives their consent ahead of time, hospitals can't disclose information about an admitted patient to their family. You could be searching for someone for days, completely unaware of the fact that they're sitting in a psych ward or a hospital bed just miles away."[2]

Eventually Megan recovered her mental faculties and found her way home, but her story shows some of the issues most people never think of until they or someone they know goes missing.

1. Ryan Menzes and Megan, "5 Horrifying Things That Happen When You Go Missing," Cracked, March 16, 2015. www.cracked.com/article_21960_5-strange-realities-being-missing-person.html.

2. Menzes and Megan, "5 Horrifying Things That Happen When You Go Missing."

city held a funeral for Precious Doe. Hundreds who never knew her when she was alive attended.

A nice funeral was not enough for local comic book artist Alonzo Washington, however. The father of seven children, he had been haunted by the case ever since he heard the story of Precious Doe's remains being found. He began a campaign to get the word out about the little girl, using every means possible. He held candlelight vigils, paid for ads about her death in newspapers, raised more than $33,000 in reward money for tips leading to her identity, and even created a comic book about the little girl—but without success. "No one in her family was claiming her," Washington said to explain his involvement. "This little girl had no other champion."[76]

As months and years went by without any clue to the little girl's identity, Washington always put an ad in several newspapers on the anniversary of Precious Doe's discovery. On April 30, 2005, more than four years after her murder, someone came forward. It turned out to be an older man from Muskegee, Oklahoma, who said the little girl could be his great-granddaughter, whom he had not seen in four years.

The man was right. His grandson, Harrell Johnson, was living with the child's mother when the murder occurred. Johnson and Precious Doe's mother later married. It was Johnson who killed the little girl, whose name was Erica Michelle Maria Green, by kicking her in the head when she did not want to go to bed when he told her to. Johnson was high on a drug called PCP at the time. Erica's mother

Michelle testified against her husband. She said that after killing Erica, he beheaded her, hoping to make it harder for anyone to identify her.

Johnson was found guilty of murder and was sentenced to life in prison. Though Washington's publicity about the case was successful in solving it, he was happy only because Precious Doe finally had a name. "There were times when I despaired," he admitted. "But this case wouldn't let me go. Every kid deserves better than to end up in a trash bag."[77]

A Constant Reminder

Advances in technology have given the police better tools to find the missing, but it is still difficult to hear what happens to those who go missing, especially when a case takes a turn for the worse. Police investigators understand, however, that when a person goes missing, it affects everyone around them. For the missing person's family, it is better to get an answer—even a hard one—than to live years in limbo, wondering if the person will ever come home.

For Stark, the information received about the young children and teens who go missing is especially difficult:

It's a constant reminder of what kind of bad stuff is out there. It affects you every day. I feel like

what we do is an important job, but it does take a toll on you. You know, you have a family and you try very hard to make things good for your kids, to give them a happy life. And most parents do that, but in my job you see an awful lot of broken families. Nothing is working. And then you investigate a case where a kid takes off and later is found dead. You go to the funerals of these kids, and you think to yourself, they're never coming back—it's over for them.[78]

However, the difficulties of the job highlight for Stark the importance of spending time with his own children:

You go home after working on cases like these—you don't just pop a beer and sit in front of the TV to watch sports, you know? If my kid says, "Hey Dad, can you build LEGOs with me?" I do. The answer is always yes. You think about what's important, because you know too much of what is possible. You know things can change in an instant.[79]

Notes

Introduction: Danger

1. "The National Missing and Unidentified Persons System, University of North Texas Center for Human Identification," accessed September 19, 2017. www.untfsu.com/namus.html.

Chapter One: Gone

2. Quoted in Kanyakrit Vongkiatkajorn, "NYPD: How The Police Handles Missing Persons Cases," The Missing: Searching for New York's Lost. themissingny.nycitynewsservice. com/part-two/nypd-explainer/.

3. Cathe Carbone, interview by Gail B. Stewart, June 4, 2010.

4. Carbone, interview, June 4, 2010.

5. Carbone, interview, June 4, 2010.

6. Chris Stark, interview by Gail B. Stewart, May 27, 2010.

7. Stark, interview, May 27, 2010.

8. Stark, interview, May 27, 2010.

9. Stark, interview, May 27, 2010.

10. Stark, interview, May 27, 2010.

11. Stark, interview, May 27, 2010.

12. Stark, interview, May 27, 2010.

13. Stark, interview, May 27, 2010.

14. Brady Harrison, interview by Gail B. Stewart, July 15, 2010.

15. Harrison, interview, July 15, 2010.

16. Harrison, interview, July 15, 2010.

17. Stark, interview, May 27, 2010.

18. Stark, interview, May 27, 2010.

19. Quoted in Tony Aiello, "Girl, 3, Wanders from Home, Freezes to Death," CBS New York, February 5, 2009. wcbstv.com/local/moun-taindale.child.freezes.2.926994. html.

20. Quoted in Alexis Weed, "Teen Drove into Ditch, Vanished as Parents Searched," CNN, January 18, 2010. www.cnn.com/2010/CRIME/01/18/grace.coldcase.swanson/index.html.

21. Quoted in Weed, "Teen Drove into Ditch."

22. Ken Anderson, interview by Gail B. Stewart, June 1, 2010.

23. Anderson, interview, June 1, 2010.

24. Anderson, interview, June 1, 2010.

25. Quoted in Weed, "Teen Drove into Ditch."

26. Anderson, interview, June 1, 2010.

27. Sarah Ryan, telephone interview by Gail B. Stewart, June 15, 2010.

Chapter Two: Deliberately Missing

28. Maya, interview by Gail B. Stewart, August 1, 2010.

29. Ann Rivera, telephone interview by Gail B. Stewart, July 14, 2010.

30. Mike Sullivan, interview by Gail B. Stewart, June 11, 2010.

31. Sullivan, interview, June 11, 2010.

32. Benny Williams, interview by Gail B. Stewart, June 16, 2010.

33. Chris Stark, interview by Gail B. Stewart, June 16, 2010.

34. Sullivan, interview, June 11, 2010.

35. Mark, telephone interview by Gail B. Stewart, August 1, 2010.

36. Mark, telephone interview, August 1, 2010.

37. Sullivan, interview, June 11, 2010.

38. Sullivan, interview, June 11, 2010.

39. Sullivan, interview, June 11, 2010.

40. Stark, interview, June 16, 2010.

41. Sullivan, interview, June 11, 2010.

42. Stark, interview, May 27, 2010.

43. Stark, interview, May 27, 2010.

44. Stark, interview, May 27, 2010.

45. Stark, interview, May 27, 2010.

46. Stark, interview, May 27, 2010.

47. Quoted in Cristina Corbin, "Parents Plead for Ohio Teen's Return After Cops Charge Boyfriend with Hampering Investigation," Fox News, June 27, 2010. www.foxnews.com/us/2010/06/27/police-charge-missing-ohio-teens-boyfriend-obstruction-justice.

48. Stark, interview, May 27, 2010.

49. Stark, interview, May 27, 2010.

Chapter Three: Taken

50. Rivera, telephone interview, July 14, 2010.

51. Stark, interview, May 27, 2010.

52. Quoted in "Amber Hagerman," TRUtv. www.trutv.com/library/crime/notorious_murders/famous/amber_hagerman/1_index.html.

53. Wallace, telephone interview by Gail B. Stewart, June 30, 2010.

54. Hannah McGill, interview by Gail B. Stewart, August 2, 2010.

55. Quoted in Christopher Leonard, "Teen Called Hero for Missing-Boy Tip," *Washington Post*, January 17, 2007. www.washingtonpost.com/wp-dyn/content/article/2007/01/16/AR2007011601041.html.

56. Quoted in "Kidnapped: Shawn Hornbeck's Incredible Story," CBS News, September 24, 2008. www.cbsnews.com/stories/2008/09/24/48hours/main4474670.shtml.

Chapter Four: No Body?

57. Paul Zech, telephone interview by Gail B. Stewart, August 26, 2010.

58. Quoted in Dolly Stolze, "Cold Case Chronicles: The Acid Bath Murders," *Forensic Magazine*, March 15, 2017. www.forensicmag.com/article/2017/03/cold-case-chronicles-acid-bath-murders.

59. Erwin Vermeij, "The Acid Test: Can You Dissolve a Body Completely?," *New Scientist*, November 5, 2014. www.newscientist.com/article/mg22429940.900-the-acid-test-can-you-dissolve-a-body-completely/.

60. Vermeij, "The Acid Test."

61. Quoted in Connie Fletcher, *Every Contact Leaves a Trace: Crime Scene Experts Talk About Their Work from Discovery Through Verdict*. New York, NY: St. Martin's, 2006, pp. 27–28.

62. Quoted in Fletcher, *Every Contact Leaves a Trace*, p. 28.

63. Quoted in Fletcher, *Every Contact Leaves a Trace*, pp. 29–30.

64. Quoted in Ward Harkavy, "The Searchers: These Scientists and Cops Dig Deep for the Truth. Sometimes They Unearth More," *Westword*, April 5, 1995. www.westword.com/content/printVersion/207667.

65. Quoted in Harkavy, "The Searchers."

66. Quoted in Rebecca McQuilla, "On the Trail of the Body Hunters The Police Were Sure They Knew the Killer but There Could Be No Murder Case Without a Body, and No Peace for the Family of Missing Michele Wallace. That's Where a Group of Pioneering Volunteers Came In," redOrbit, November 4, 2005. www.red-orbit.com/news/science/295039/on_the_trail_of_the_body_hunters_the_police_were.

67. Quoted in McQuilla, "On the Trail of the Body Hunters."

**Chapter Five:
Starting with J. Doe**

68. Stark, interview, May 27, 2010.

69. Wallace, telephone interview, June 30, 2010.

70. Michael McGee, interview by Gail B. Stewart, June 4, 2009.

71. Quoted in Lewis Kamb, "People Go Missing, Killers Go Free," *Seattle Post-Intelligencer*, February 17, 2003. www.seattlepi.com/local/108579_missingday17.shtml.

72. Quoted in Kamb, "People Go Missing."

73. Kamb, "People Go Missing."

74. Quoted in Fletcher, *Every Contact Leaves a Trace*, p. 198.

75. Quoted in Doug Page, "Internet Databases Help Police Solve Missing Persons Cases," *Dayton Daily News*, February 27, 2010. www.daytondailynews.com/news/crime--law/internet-databases-help-police-solve-missing-persons-cases/sfvIbF-wRXhLCaH7mQV0PQL/.

76. Quoted in Bob Meadows, "Who Was Precious Doe? A Mystery Solved," *People*, May 23, 2005. www.people.com/archive/who-was-precious-doe-a-mystery-solved-vol-63-no-20/.

77. Quoted in Meadows, "Who Was Precious Doe?"

78. Stark, interview, May 27, 2010.

79. Stark, interview, May 27, 2010.

For More Information

Books

Anniss, Matt. *Cold Cases*. New York, NY: Gareth Stevens Publishing, 2014.
When a crime goes unsolved for many years, it is called a "cold case." Scientists who try to solve cold cases must use different methods than those who have fresh evidence to work with, and this book details those methods.

Fletcher, Connie. *Every Contact Leaves a Trace: Crime Scene Experts Talk About Their Work from Discovery Through Verdict*. New York, NY: St. Martin's, 2006.
This book contains information from Fletcher's interviews with unidentified detectives, crime scene specialists, lawyers, and medical examiners.

Jackson, Steve. *No Stone Unturned: The True Story of NecroSearch International, the World's Premier Forensic Investigators*. New York, NY: Kensington, 2002.
A great resource for readers, this book details the disappearance, search, and eventual recovery of several missing persons and shows the amazing tools used by the forensic pioneers of NecroSearch.

Duke, Shirley. *STEAM Jobs in Forensics*. North Mankato, MN: Rourke Educational Media, 2017.
Forensic scientists rely on skills they learned in classes that deal with STEAM subjects to perform many different kinds of jobs. From analyzing evidence to reconstructing a face, forensic scientists must use their knowledge of science, technology, engineering, art, and math.

Morewitz, Stephen J., and Caroline Sturdy Colls, eds. *Handbook of Missing Persons*. Switzerland: Springer, 2016.
This collection of articles by various forensic experts details recent forensic science advancements.

Websites

Doe Network (www.doenetwork.org)

This is the website of a national volunteer organization dedicated to helping law enforcement identify missing persons and unnamed victims. It contains composite sketches and offers ways the public can get more involved.

Federal Bureau of Investigation: Kidnappings and Missing Persons (www.fbi.gov/wanted/kidnap)

This website gives photos and important information about people who are currently missing or believed to be kidnapped.

The Missing: Searching for New York's Lost (themissingny.nycitynewsservice.com)

A product of NYCity News Service at the CUNY Graduate School of Journalism and the investigative news publication City Limits, this website has a collection of stories about various missing individuals and those who search for them.

National Runaway Safeline (www.1800runaway.org)

This website is a reference for children and young adults who have run away or who are considering running away. Of note is the collected data from surveys the Safeline has conducted with runaways.

The Vanished (www.stitcher.com/podcast/the-vanished-podcast)

Each episode of this free podcast explores a different missing persons case. Some are from years ago, while others are very recent. Anyone who has information in any of these cases is encouraged to let the police know.

Index

Picture Credits

About the Author

Amanda Vink is a writer and actress from Buffalo, NY. She graduated from SUNY Fredonia with a bachelor's degree in English and creative writing. When she is not writing, Amanda enjoys planning adventures to new locations and learning to play the bagpipes.